Volume 19

make it yourself
The Complete Step-by-Step Library of Needlework and Crafts

COLUMBIA HOUSE/New York

Editor: Mary Harding
Assistant Editor: Margo Coughtrie
Editorial Assistants: Sally Fisher/Maureen Paton
Consultants: Greta Barrett/Angela Jeffs (Sewing)/
Patsy North (Embroidery and Crafts)/
Frances Rogers (Knitting and Crochet)
Managing Editor: Nicholas Wright
Design Co-ordinator: Jan Churcher
Production Control: Sheila Biddlecombe
Editorial Director: Graham Donaldson

© 1973/4/5/6 by Orbis-Verlag für Publizistik GMBH and Co. KG.
© 1975/6/7 Phoebus Publishing Company / BPC Publishing Ltd.

Distributed by Columbia House, 51 West 52nd Street, New York, New York 10019

Printed in U.S.A.

Introduction

By Volume 19 of Make It Yourself, even relative newcomers to knitting and crochet will have acquired the know-how to tackle some of the more advanced projects. Aran knitting is the ultimate in textured patterning and is timeless in style as you'll see from our splendid models for men and women. Knitting with several colors is not as formidable as it seems, either, once you have mastered the knack of following a chart. Try our designs and see.

Lacy crochet with intricate patterning is worth the extra effort you spend on it for the superb end result. Make the snowflake mat to begin with, then progress to a large project such as a magnificent bedspread. Learn some new techniques, too, like star stitch for a chunky jacket.

In the dressmaking section, we present a range of clothes from raincoats to practical dresses for all ages. For the children, there are some lovable hand puppets, Indian costumes, canvas bike bags, and a softly-padded nursery rug to sew.

Use simple embroidery stitches in delicate designs for stunning results. There are some crisp tablecloths, a peasant blouse, and a silk dress to decorate.

make it yourself

Contents — Page

How to use this book Body measurements chart **2312-2313**
Fashion sizing
Metric conversion
Selecting a yarn

Knitting How-to instructions **2315-2337**
Gloves
Hats
Mittens
Pullovers
Scarf
Socks
Tank tops

Crochet How-to instructions **2338-2359**
Bedspreads
Bolero
Cardigan
Hat
Jackets
Mat
Vests

Dressmaking How-to instructions **2360-2375**
Dresses
Jackets
Raincoats
Shirts
Skirts
Suits
Vests

Sewing Bicycle bags **2376-2389**
Hand puppets
Indian costumes
Patchwork quilt
Pillows
Rug
Tablecloth

Embroidery How-to instructions **2390-2409**
Blouse
Dress
Embroidery patterns
Tablecloths

Canvaswork How-to instructions **2410-2415**
Pictures
Pillows

Crafts How-to instructions **2416-2426**
Pillows
Rugs

Index **2427-2428**

Notes **2429-2432**

How to use this book..

Selecting a yarn

In this series, we are introducing a new and easy way to identify the yarn used in our knitting and crochet features! You will find an actual-size, colored photograph of the yarn given with each set of directions.

Materials Required:

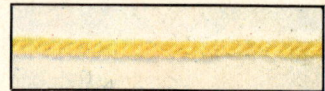

150 (200) gm or 6 (7) oz each of yellow and green, 50 gm or 2 oz blue [100 gm = 360 m or 390 yds]. Knitting needles size 4 (Am) or 10 (Eng).

At one time or another, you have probably suffered the disappointment of finding that the yarn specified in knitting and crochet directions is difficult to obtain or totally unavailable in your area. When this happens you are faced with the often impossible task of finding a substitute yarn. By matching a yarn against our photograph, you can choose a yarn of similar weight and texture from the range of yarns available in your store or favorite needlework shop.

This method is also helpful if you have yarn left over from other projects and you are unsure whether it is the proper weight or texture and whether you have sufficient yardage to finish a new shawl or pullover.

To help you determine the amount of yarn needed, we have also listed the yardage per skein for the yarn used. Most yarn companies give the yardage per skein in their sample books, and many shops have interchangeable yarn lists which give the yardages per unit weight. You will then be able to see whether you will need to make adjustments in the number of skeins required of the yarn which you have chosen.

Before you start to work the pattern, work a test swatch and match it against the Tension given in the directions (see the Tension Gauge instructions below). Adjust the needle or hook size if necessary. Any yarn which can be worked at the tension given in the directions can be used for that pattern.

Centimeters or inches?

The metric system of measurement is gaining greater use and acceptance, and some needlework and crafts equipment and materials are already sold by the metric weight and/or length. For your convenience, we have given all the weights and measures in both systems. NOTE: In some cases, the conversions are not exact. The measurements have been rounded to the nearest convenient or appropriate number.

Tension gauge

One key to successful knitting or crocheting is the tension! Each of our directions is based on the given tension gauge (number of rows and stitches to 10 cm or 4").

To check your tension, work a test piece 12 cm or 5" square in the stitch pattern. Make a cardboard template with a 10 cm or 4" square cut out of it. Place the template over your swatch and count the rows and stitches. Compare the numbers with the tension gauge given in the directions. If your swatch has too few stitches and rows, work more tightly or use smaller equipment. If you have more than the number given, use larger needles, or hook.

Directions for the items shown can be used for any yarn of similar thickness and texture, providing you can achieve the proper tension.

Do not be upset if you find that you do have to adjust the needle or hook size. This does not mean that there is anything wrong with your knitting or crocheting. The needle and hook sizes given in the directions are an average, but by no means an absolute. There is great variation in the tension at which different people work, and you will even find slight variations in the tension of your work. On days when you are tense or tired, your knitting or crocheting will probably be a little tighter.

Fashion sizing

Dressmaking

Do you know your size? Don't just say 'yes', because as you already know, the fit of pattern and ready-to-wear sizes varies.

To eliminate confusion, we have lettered our sizes (A, B, C) instead of giving them the traditional numbering (10, 12).

Remeasure yourself and match your body measurements with those given in the chart below. All of the patterns are designed according to these measurements, so choose the pattern size which is right for your measurements. You may have to make minor adjustments in the pattern pieces to adapt them to your body contours, and Dressmaking Pattern Sheet 2 explains how to do this. Other dressmaking pattern sheets will deal with more complex fitting for specific garments such as pants.

DO NOT MEASURE THE PATTERNS. Every pattern includes, according to the design, an added measure to allow for easy movement when wearing the garment. Just compare your body measurements with the measurements given in the chart and choose the proper size.

Each pattern is given in five sizes. Two of the sizes are given on the pattern sheet and the other three sizes can be easily drawn from the two sizes given. Directions for adapting for the three additional sizes are given on each pattern sheet. Even if you are not one of the standard pattern sizes, but are a mixed size made up of several standard measurements, you can still use our patterns. Since each pattern can be adapted for five sizes – a size smaller, a size larger, and a size between the two sizes actually marked on the pattern sheet – it is possible to construct a pattern for yourself. Directions for constructing a mixed-size pattern are given on Dressmaking Pattern Sheet 2.

Knitting and Crochet

The knitting and crochet sizes are based on the Dressmaking Body Measurements Chart. For each direction, you will be given the actual body measurements for which the garment is intended. The finished knitted or crocheted garment will be larger than the given measurements to allow for comfort and movement.

Size: Directions are for 92 cm (36") bust. Changes for 96, 100 cm (37½", 39½") bust are in brackets.

Do you know your size?

Don't just say 'yes'. Remeasure yourself, following the diagrams and instructions, and then check the Body Measurements chart.

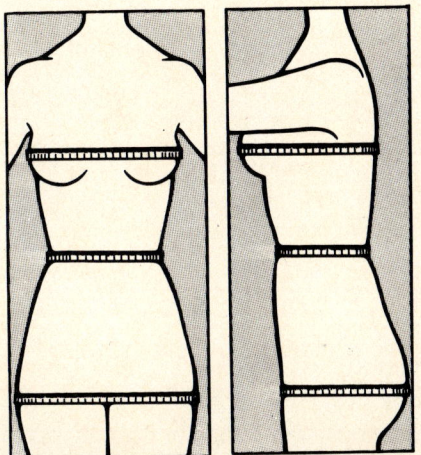

Bust – measure around the fullest part of the bust.
Waist – tie a string around your body so that it settles comfortably at your natural waistline. Measure your waist at the string.
Hips – measure around the fullest part of your hips (this generally falls 7"–9" below your waistline).

Important hints:
When taking measurements, do not hold the tape measure slack or pull it too tight. The tape must lie evenly horizontal all around the body – it should not go up at the back and down at the front. You will find it simpler and more accurate to be measured by someone else.

Body measurements chart

WOMEN

Size	A	B	C	D	E	F	G	H
Bust	80 cm (31½")	84 cm (33")	88 cm (34½")	92 cm (36")	96 cm (37½")	100 cm (39½")	104 cm (41")	108 cm (42½")
Waist	59 cm (23¼")	63.5 cm (25")	68 cm (26½")	72.5 cm (28½")	77 cm (30½")	81.5 cm (32")	86 cm (34")	90 cm (35½")
Hips	86 cm (34")	90 cm (35½")	94 cm (37")	98 cm (38½")	102 cm (40")	106 cm (42")	110 cm (43½")	114 cm (45")

MEN

Size	J	K	L	M	N	O	P	Q
Chest	84 cm (33")	88 cm (34½")	92 cm (36")	96 cm (37½")	100 cm (39½")	104 cm (41")	108 cm (42½")	112 cm (44")
Hip	88 cm (34½")	92 cm (36")	96 cm (37½")	100 cm (39½")	104 cm (41")	108 cm (42½")	112 cm (44")	116 cm (45½")
Neck	36 cm (14")	37 cm (14½")	38 cm (15")	39 cm (15½")	40 cm (15¾")	41 cm (16")	42 cm (16½")	43 cm (17")
Arm	60 cm (23¾")	61 cm (24")	62 cm (24¼")	63 cm (24¾")	64 cm (25¼")	65 cm (25½")	66 cm (26")	67 cm (26½")

CHILDREN

Size	S	T	U	V	W	X	Y	Z
Height	110 cm (43")	116 cm (45½")	122 cm (48")	128 cm (50½")	134 cm (52¾")	140 cm (55")	146 cm (57½")	152 cm (60")
Chest	60 cm (23¾")	62 cm (24¼")	64 cm (25¼")	66 cm (26")	68 cm (26¾")	70 cm (27½")	73 cm (28¾")	76 cm (29¾")
Waist	58 cm (23")	59 cm (23¼")	60 cm (23¾")	61 cm (24")	62 cm (24¼")	63 cm (24¾")	64 cm (25¼")	65 cm (25¾")
Hips	66 cm (26")	68 cm (26¾")	70 cm (27½")	72 cm (28¼")	74 cm (29")	76 cm (29¾")	80 cm (31½")	84 cm (33")

Knitting
The ultimate in warmth

The classic Aran sweater – an outstanding cold-weather companion.

The handsome Aran style looks equally effective on both men and women and will prove invaluable in any wardrobe. The warm pull-on hat is in the same yarn.

FOR BOTH
Basic Pattern: See Knitting Diagram. Only half of the pattern is given, the other half is worked in reverse, from left to right. The diagram shows the first wrong side R in which sts are increased, after that, only the right side R are shown. Work all wrong side R as the sts present themselves. For the Large Diamond Pattern, repeat R 2–29; for Center Cable Pattern, repeat R 2–25.

Double Moss Stitch Pattern: (worked at sides of Back and Front) K 1, P 1 rib for 2 R, then P 1, K 1 rib for 2 R. Repeat the 4 R.

Border Pattern: R 1: (wrong side) Alternately K 1, P 1 into back of st. R 2: Alternately K 1 into back of st, P 1. Repeat R 1 and 2.

Tension: (measured without stretching) 18 sts and 20 R = 10 cm or 4".

Abbreviations: K = knit. P = purl. St(s) = stitch(es). St st = stocking or stockinette stitch. R = row(s).

WOMAN'S SET
Size: Directions are for 92 cm or 36" bust. Changes for 97 cm or 38" bust are in brackets.

Materials Required:

[100 gm = 90 m or 100 yds.] Sweater: 1200 (1300) gm or 43 (46) oz white. Knitting needles size 10½ (Am) or 2 (Eng). Stitch holder. Cable needle. Hat: 100 gm or 4 oz each red and white. Knitting needles size 15 (Am) or 000 (Eng).

DIRECTIONS
Back: Using finer needles, cast on 76 (82) sts and work 8 cm or 3¼" in Border Pattern, then work from Knitting Diagram, beginning R 1 with 4 (7) sts in Double Moss St Pattern, then repeat the Knitting Diagram

2315

from right to left and then from left to right, and work last 4 (7) sts in Double Moss St — 82 (88) sts. Work from Diagram, repeating R 2–29 for Diamond Pattern and R 2–25 for Cable Pattern, keeping a border of Double Moss St each end. Work straight to 53 (52) cm or 21" (20½"). **Shape Armholes:** At beginning of every R, cast off 3 sts 2 times, 2 sts 4 times, 1 st 4 (6) times — 64 (68) sts. Work straight to 72 cm or 28¼". **Shape Neck and Shoulders:** Cast off center 26 sts and work on each side separately. At neck edge, in every 2nd R cast off 3 sts 1 time and 2 sts 1 time. *At the same time,* at armhole edge, in every 2nd R cast off 7 (8) sts 2 times.
Front: Work as for Back to 64 cm or 25¼".
Shape Neck: Cast off center 10 sts and work on each side separately. At neck edge, in every 2nd R cast off 3 sts 1 time, 2 sts 2 times, and 1 st 6 times. *At the same time,* when armhole measures same as Back to shoulder, in every 2nd R at armhole edge cast off 7 (8) sts 2 times.
Sleeves: Cast on 36 (40) sts and work 8 cm or 3¼" in Border Pattern, then follow Knitting Diagram, but begin R 1 at the 17th (15th) st, work to end of Diagram, then work Diagram in reverse over next 18 (20) sts — 40 (44) sts. Continue in pattern as set, increasing 1 st each end of every 6th R (alternately every 4th and 6th R) 12 (14) times, working increased sts into pattern where possible — 64 (72) sts. Work straight to 47 cm or 18½".
Shape Top: At beginning of every R, cast off 5 (6) sts 2 times, 3 sts 2 times, 2 sts 4 times, 1 st 10 times, 2 sts 4 times, 3 sts 2 times, and 5 (6) sts 2 times. Cast off remaining 6 (10) sts.
Finishing: Join right shoulder seam. With the right side facing, pick up and K 78 sts around neck and work in Border Pattern for 36 cm or 14⅛". Cast off in rib. Join all seams.
Hat: Use all yarn double throughout. Using thicker needles and white, cast on 46 sts and K 1 R. Change to red and K 2 R. Now change to reverse st st and work with 1 strand each of red and white to 10 cm or 4". Change to st st and work *2 cm or ¾" in mixed yarns, 5 cm or 2" in white, repeat from * 1 time, then continue in mixed yarns to 25 cm or 9¾".
Shape Top: In next R, K together every 4th and 5th st — 37 sts. In the next 3 R, K together the decreased st with previous st, thus taking off 9 sts in each R. Cut strands and draw through remaining sts. With P side as right side, join seams, reversing lower 10 cm or 4" for turn-back.

MAN'S SWEATER
Size: Directions are for 97 cm or 38" chest. Changes for 102 cm or 40" chest are in brackets.
Materials Required: Yarn: (see sample for Woman's Set) 1400 (1500) gm or 50 (53) oz white. Knitting needles size 10½ (Am) or 2 (Eng). Cable needle. Stitch holder.

DIRECTIONS
Back: Cast on 82 (88) sts and work 10 cm or 4" in Border Pattern, then work from Knitting Diagram, beginning R 1 with 7 (10) sts in Double Moss St Pattern, then repeat the Knitting Diagram from right to left and from left to right, and work the last 7 (10) sts in Double Moss St — 88 (94) sts. Work from Diagram, with Double Moss Stitch each end, to 53 cm or 21".
Shape Armholes: At beginning of every R, cast off 3 sts 2 times, 2 sts 4 (6) times, 1 st 6 (4) times — 68 (72) sts. Work straight to 75 cm or 29½".
Shape Neck and Shoulders: Cast off center 26 sts and work on each side separately. At neck edge, in every 2nd R cast off 3 sts 1 time and 2 sts 1 time. *At the same time,* at armhole edge, in every 2nd R cast off 5 (6) sts 2 times and 6 (6) sts 1 time.
Front: Work as for Back to 67 cm or 26½".
Shape Neck: Cast off center 10 sts and work on each side separately. At neck edge, in every 2nd R cast off 3 sts 1 time, 2 sts 2 times, and 1 st 6 times. *At the same time,* shape shoulder as for Back.
Sleeves: Cast on 38 sts and work 10 cm or 4" in Border Pattern, then follow Diagram, but begin R 1 at the 16th st and work to end of Diagram, then work from Diagram in reverse — 42 sts. Continue in pattern as set, increasing 1 st alternately in every 4th and 6th R 14 times (every 4th R 12 times and every 6th R 4 times) — 70 (74) sts. Work straight to 48 cm or 19".
Shape Top: At beginning of every R cast off 5 (6) sts 2 times, 3 sts 2 times, 2 sts 4 times, 1 st 14 times, 2 sts 4 times, 3 sts 2 times, and 5 (6) sts 2 times. Cast off remaining 8 sts.
Finishing: As Woman's Sweater, but pick up and K 88 sts at neck edge and only work 26 cm or 10¼".

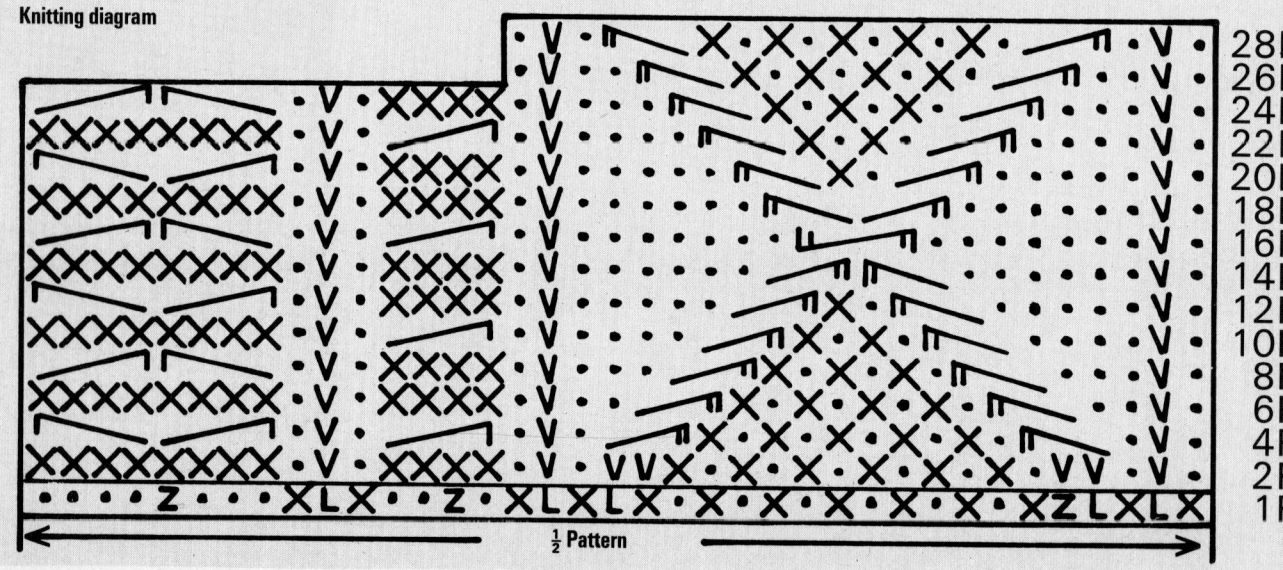

Knitting diagram

½ Pattern

2316

Here you can see a close-up of the design on both sweaters. The bold diamond shapes offset the intricate cable patterns.

X = Knit
• = Purl
V = Knit into back of stitch
L = Purl into back of stitch
Z = Pick up horizontal thread and purl into back

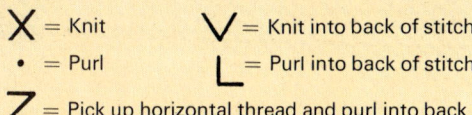 = Transfer 2 sts onto cable needle at front of work, purl next stitch, knit into backs of sts on cable needle

= Place 1 st on cable needle behind work, knit into backs of next 2 sts, purl st on cable needle

= Place 2 sts on cable needle behind work, knit into backs of next 2 sts, knit into backs of sts on cable needle

= Place 2 sts on cable needle behind work, knit next 2 sts, knit sts on cable needle

= Place 2 sts on cable needle at front of work, knit next 2 sts, knit sts on cable needle

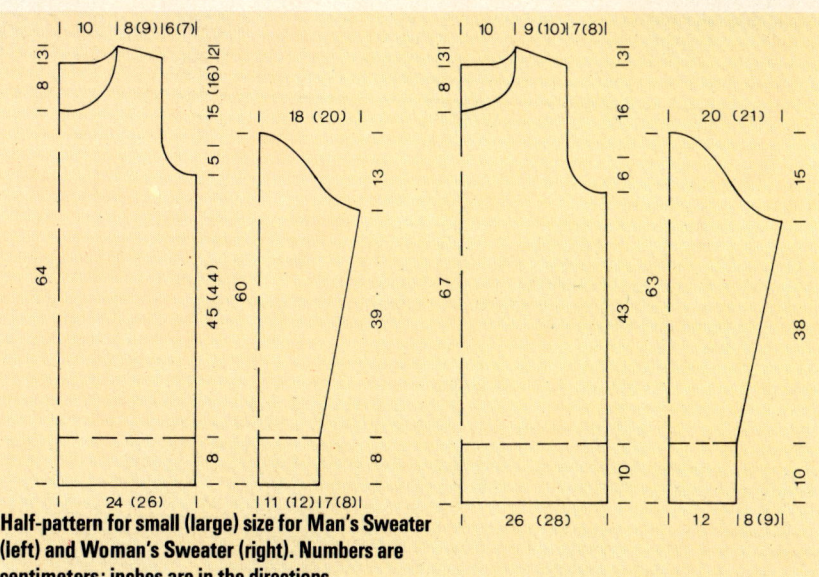

Half-pattern for small (large) size for Man's Sweater (left) and Woman's Sweater (right). Numbers are centimeters; inches are in the directions.

Double cream

Here are two pullovers in the Aran idiom. The round-neck version has an all-over plait pattern and shoulder yokes, while the V-neck style has ribbed sleeves and sides.

Both Styles

Size: Directions are for 84 cm or 33" bust. Changes for 92 cm or 36" bust are in brackets.

Materials Required:

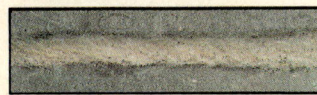

700 (800) gm or 25 (29) oz white [100 gm = 105 m or 115 yds]. Knitting needles sizes 10 and 10½ (Am) or 2 and 4 (Eng). Cable needle.

Basic Stitch: See Knitting Diagram below.

Crossing 2 + 1 st to the right: K 3rd st at front, then K 1st and 2nd sts.

Crossing 1 + 2 sts to the left: Place 1st st onto cable needle at front, K next 2 sts, then K st from cable needle.

Tension: 15 sts and 20 R = 10 cm or 4".

V-neck Style

Back: Using finer needles, cast on 66 (74) sts and work 12 cm or 4¾" in K 1, P 1 rib. Change to thicker needles, placing sts in R 1 (wrong side) thus: K 1 (edge st), rib 9 (13) sts, repeat sts 1–18 of Knitting Diagram 2 times, sts 1–10 1 time, rib 9 (13) sts, K 1 (edge st). Work straight in pattern to 36 cm or 14".

Shape Armholes: At beginning of every R, cast off 3 sts 2 times, 2 sts 4 times, and 1 st 4 times — 48 (56) sts. Work straight to 53 (54) cm or 20¾" (21¼").

Shape Neck and Shoulders: Cast off center 22 sts and work on each side separately. At neck edge, in every 2nd R cast off 2 sts 1 time and 1 st 1 time. *At the same time,* at 54 (55) cm or 21¼" (21¾") at armhole edge, cast off 5 (7) sts 2 times.

Front: Work as for Back to 35 (36) cm or 13¾" (14¼").

Shape Neck: Divide work at center and work on each side separately. At 36 cm or 14" for both sizes, shape armhole as for Back. *At the same time,* decrease 1 st at neck edge in every R 6 times. (To decrease at right side of Right Front, K 1, then slip 1, K 1, pass slip st over. On wrong side, P 2 together before edge st. On Left Front before edge st, K 2 together and on wrong side R slip 1, P 1, pass slip st over.) Now at neck edge, decrease 1 st every 2nd R 5 times, then 1 st every 4th R 3 times. Shape shoulder at 54 (55) cm or 21¼" (21¾") as for Back.

Sleeves: Using finer needles, cast on 32 (36) sts and work 8 cm or 3" in K 1, P 1 rib. Continue in rib, increasing 1 st each end of every 8th R 8 times — 50 (54) sts. Work straight to 45 cm or 17¾".

Shape Top: At beginning of every R, cast off 3 (4) sts 2 times, 2 sts 4 times, 1 st 14 times, 2 sts 2 times, 3 (4) sts 2 times. Cast off.

Neckband: Using finer needles, cast on 99 sts and work 4 cm or 1½" in K 1, P 1 rib. Cast off in rib.

Finishing: Join seams. Sew on Neckband, crossing it right over left at front.

Round-neck Style

Back: Work rib as for other style. Change to thicker needles, work thus: R 1: K 1 (edge st) K 1, repeat sts 1 (15)–18 of Knitting Diagram 1 time, sts 1–18 2 (3) times, sts 1–8 (12) 1 time, K 1, then K 1 (edge st). Continue in pattern as set and work as other style to neck edge in every R 6 times. Shape Shoulders: At beginning of every R, cast off 7 (9) sts 4 times. Cast off.

Front: Work as for Back to 45 (46) cm or 17¾" (18").

Shape Neck: Cast off center 10 sts and work on each side separately. At neck edge, in every 2nd R cast off 3 (4) sts 2 times and 2 sts 2 times. *At the same time,* at 50 (51) cm or 19¾" (20") at armhole edge, in every 2nd R cast off 4 (5) sts 1 time, 5 (6) sts 1 time.

Right Sleeve: Using finer needles, cast on 32 (36) sts and work 8 cm or 3" in K 1, P 1 rib, increasing 1 st each end of last R — 34 (38) sts. Change to thicker needles and work in Basic Stitch, placing sts thus: R 1: (wrong side) K 1 (edge st), work sts 17 (15)–18 1 time, sts 1–18 1 time, sts 1–12 (14) 1 time, K 1 (edge st). Continue as for Sleeve of other style until 12 sts remain. Work in pattern on these 12 sts for 6 (7) cm or 2½" (2¾")**, ending after a wrong side R. At beginning of next R, cast off 6 sts 1 time, then every 2nd R cast off 3 (2) sts 2 (3) times.

Left Sleeve: Work as for Right Sleeve to ** and end after a right side R. Match Right Sleeve to completion.

Neckband: Using finer needles, cast on 78 sts and work 3 cm or 1¼" in K 1, P 1 rib. Cast off in rib.

Finishing: Join seams, then sew on Neckband.

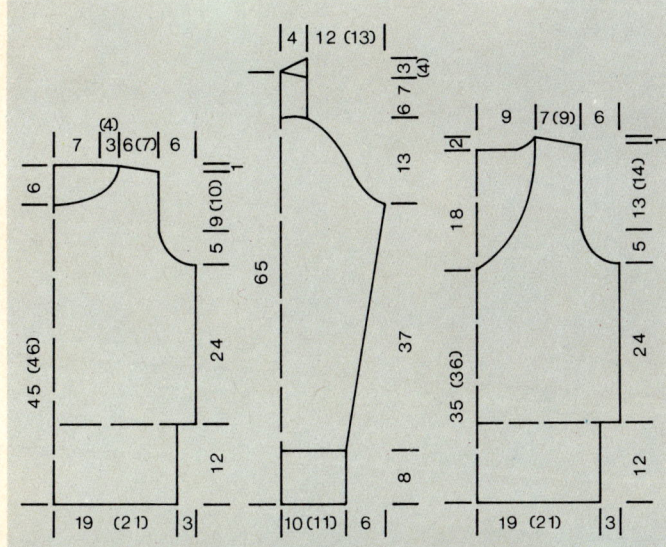

Half-pattern in small (large) size for Round-neck Style on the left, Sleeve in the center, and V-neck Style on the right. The numbers are centimeters; inches are in the directions.

Knitting Diagram: The sts are shown as seen from the right side.
× = Knit
• = Purl
╱ = Crossing 2 and 1 sts to the right
╲ = Crossing 1 and 2 sts to the left

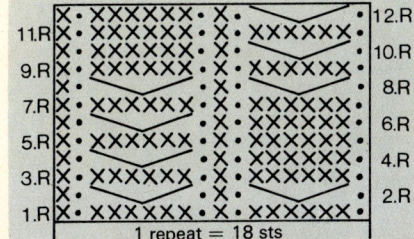

2319

Three-way coverage

Make a dramatic impact on the winter scene in our stunning threesome. Mixed yarn forms a random pattern on the scarf and an unusual background for the striking snowflake and diamond pattern on the matching pull-on hat and gloves.

Size: Hat: For head size 54 cm or 21"–21½". Scarf: 200 cm or 78" (without fringes).

Materials Required:

80 gm or 3 oz each in mixed yarn and plain white, 40 gm or 2 oz blue [40 gm = 220 m or 250 yds]. Knitting needles, 5 double-pointed needles, a long and a short circular needle size 2 (Am) or 11 (Eng).

Basic Stitch: St st. (When working in rnds, K each rnd.)

Knitting Chart: See below.

Tension: 26 sts and 38 R or rnds = 10 cm or 4".

Abbreviations: K = knit. P = purl. St(s) = stitch(es). St st = stocking or stockinette stitch. R = row(s). Rnd(s) = round(s).

SCARF

Using mixed yarn and the pair of needles, cast on 36 sts, and work 200 cm or 78" in st st for center strip. Cast off.

Using the long circular needle and navy, pick up and K 520 sts along each long edge. Working back and forth, K 2 R navy, 2 R st st in white, K 2 R navy, then continue in K 1, P 1 rib in white for 2 cm or ¾". Cast off. Cut navy strands 40 cm or 16" long and knot groups of 4 strands into scarf ends.

HAT

Using the short circular needle and white, cast on 144 sts and work in rnds of K 1, P 1 rib for 2 cm or ¾". K 1 rnd, P 1 rnd navy; K 2 rnds white; K 1 rnd, P 1 rnd navy; K 2 rnds mixed yarn. Now K the 11 rnds of Knitting Chart, repeating the 18 sts 8 times in each rnd. K 2 rnds mixed yarn. K 1 rnd, P 1 rnd navy; K 2 rnds white; K 1 rnd, P 1 rnd navy. Work 4 cm or 1½" in white in K 1, P 1 rib. Turn piece to other side for crown and work in white st st to 24 cm or 9½". K together every 11th and 12th st in next rnd – 132 sts. Repeat in every 2nd R 10 times with 1 st less between decreases – 12 sts. Draw up and fasten off.

GLOVES

Using double-pointed needles and white, cast on 48 sts (12 sts on each of 4 needles) and work 7 cm or 2¾" in K 1, P 1 rib. Work rnds of navy, white, navy as for Hat. Continue in mixed yarn in st st (the design is embroidered on later).

Shape for Thumb: Increase by knitting into back of thread before 1st st of 1st needle on next rnd. Increase 2 sts on every 3rd Rnd 7 times, working next increase either side of 1st increase, then following increases before and after thumb sts – 63 sts.

When 23 mixed-yarn rnds have been worked, transfer the 15 Thumb sts to safety pin. Over the opening, cast on 2 sts and work over the 50 sts, working rnds of navy, white, navy. Change to white; work fingers.

4th (little) Finger: Take 6 sts from back of hand and 6 sts from front (for right hand from 3rd and 4th needle – and for left hand from 2nd and 1st needle). Cast on 2 sts between the 2 sets of 6 sts where 4th Finger will meet 3rd Finger. Divide the 14 sts onto 3 needles and work in rnds for 4.5 cm or 1¾". Shape tip by K 2 together at beginning of every needle for 3 rnds. Draw up remaining 5 sts and fasten off firmly. **3rd Finger:** Take 6 sts from back and palm, cast on 2 sts between 3rd and 2nd Fingers, and pick up 2 sts from base of previous finger – 16 sts. Work 5.5 cm or 2¼" straight, then shape tip by decreasing at beginning of every needle until 5 sts remain. Fasten off. **2nd Finger:** Work as for 3rd Finger. **1st Finger:** Take the remaining 7 sts from back and palm and 2 sts from base of previous finger and work 5 cm or 2". Shape tip as for 3rd Finger.

Transfer Thumb sts to needles and pick up 2 sts from base of Thumb. On the 17 sts, work 2 rnds navy as before, then work in white to 4 cm or 1½". Shape tip as 3rd Finger. With navy and Swiss darning or duplicate stitch, work center motif and 2 diamond patterns.

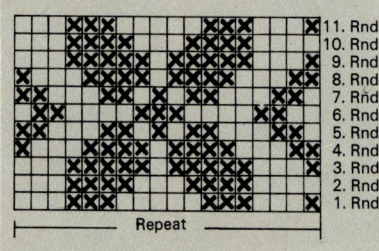

Knitting Chart: Each square = 1 stitch. Each cross = 1 stitch in blue yarn. 1 repeat of 18 stitches is given. Follow the chart when embroidering the gloves.

Knitting

Hat and mitten sets

A snug fit

Use really large needles to knit this hat and mitten set. Stocking or stockinette stitch is used throughout in three colors.

Size: Hat fits an average-sized head. Mittens fit all sizes.

Materials Required:

200 gm or 8 oz blue *or* brown, 100 gm or 4 oz in each of red and white *or* beige and white [100 gm = 112 m or 122 yds]. Knitting needles size 10½ (Am) or 2 (Eng).

Basic Stitch: St st, following the Color Chart.

Rib Pattern: K 1, P 1 rib.

Tension: 12 sts and 16 R = 10 cm or 4".

Abbreviations: K = knit. P = purl. St(s) = stitch(es). R = row(s). St st = stocking or stockinette stitch.

DIRECTIONS

Mittens: Right Hand: Using blue or brown, cast on 24 sts and follow Color Chart, working in st st to end of R 10, in Rib Pattern to end of R 16, then in st st to R 26. In next R, K 12, slip 5 sts onto safety pin. With a scrap length of yarn, cast on 5 sts, then continue straight with main yarn on all sts following Chart until R 40 has been worked.

Shape Top: K 2 sts together, K 8, K 2 sts together 2 times, K 8, K 2 together. Continue thus, decreasing 1 st each end of every R and working 2 sts together 2 times at center 4 times more. Break yarn, draw through remaining 4 sts, and fasten off firmly.

Go back to the 5 sts on safety pin and transfer to needle, pull out scrap yarn from the 5 cast-on sts and put sts on needle, then using blue or brown yarn, increase each side of the first 5 sts by working into the horizontal threads. Continue in st st on these 12 sts for 7 cm or 2¾", ending after a P R.

In next R, K 2 together, K 2, K 2 together 2 times, K 2, K 2 together. In next R, P 2 together 4 times. Cut yarn and draw through remaining 4

The hat has a turn-back and the mittens are ribbed around the wrist for warmth and comfort.

Knitting Chart: Dot = Purl, Cross = St st in color given, Grey = White.

sts, then fasten off firmly.
Left Hand: Work as for other mitten to end of R 26. In next R, K 6, slip next 5 sts onto a safety pin and continue to match other mitten.

Hat: Using blue or brown, cast on 64 sts and work as Chart following Hat Repeat to R 12. In next R, P for turn-back (thus reversing st st) and continue to follow pattern to R 40, then work in blue or brown only, decreasing for top of crown thus: (K 6, K 2 together) 8 times. P next R. In next R, (K 5, K 2 together) 8 times. P next R. In next R, (K 4, K 2 together) 8 times. Continue decreasing in every K R, working 1 st less between decreases until 8 sts remain, then K 2 together 4 times. Break yarn and draw through sts, pull up tightly.

▶ The pattern and design are the same – only the colors are different. A very subtle effect is achieved by using a combination of brown, beige, and white.

Knitting Chart: Dot =Purl, Cross =St st.
Brown =Brown, Rust =Beige, Gold =White.

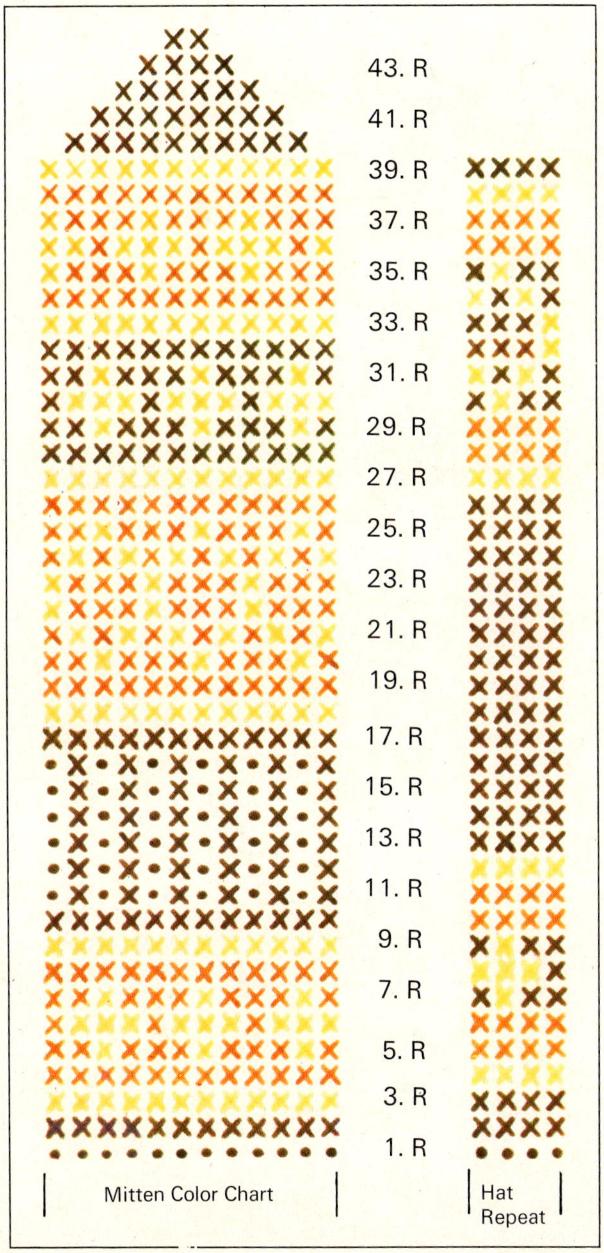

| Mitten Color Chart | Hat Repeat |

2323

How-to

Cross-stitch on knitting

Cross-stitch worked over knitted stitches can be altered to produce different sizes and shapes.

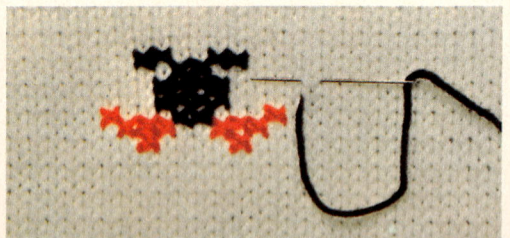

1 For the pullover on the right, we've made the cross-stitches 1 st wide and 1 R high. Because of the shape of the knitted stitch, the cross is wider than it is high.

2 In this example, each cross-stitch is 1 st wide and 2 R high. This makes the crosses higher than they are wide, giving the pattern an elongated effect.

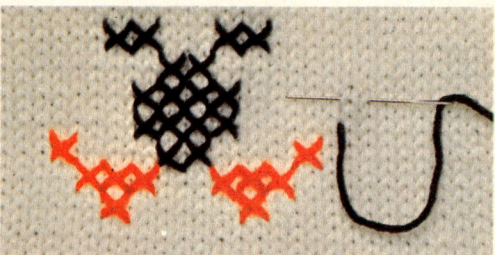

3 To make the crosses square, make each cross-stitch 1½ sts wide and 2 R high. In this case, the height is the same as in photograph 2 and the width has been altered to make it square. This will produce a design which looks exactly like the chart.

Size: Directions are for 88 cm or 33" bust. Changes for 92 cm or 36" bust are in brackets.

Materials Required:

450 (500) gm or 16 (18) oz white [50 gm = 120 m or 131 yds]. Knitting needles and circular needles sizes 4 and 5 (Am) or 8 and 9 (Eng). Tapestry yarn: 9 skeins red, 4 skeins black. St holders.

Basic Stitch: St st.
Embroidery Chart: 1 repeat of pattern is shown. Every cross = 1 cross-stitch, 1 st wide and 1 R high.
Tension: 21 sts and 27 R = 10 cm or 4".
Abbreviations: K = knit. P = purl. St(s) = stitch(es). R = row(s). St st = stocking or stockinette st. Rnd(s) = round(s).

DIRECTIONS

Back: Using finer needles and white, cast on 92 (100) sts and work 12 cm or 4¾" in K 2, P 2 rib. Change to thicker needles and work in st st to 33 (34) cm or 13" (13½").
Shape Armholes: At beginning of next 2 R cast off 4 (6) sts. Leave remaining 84 (88) sts on spare needle.
Front: Work as for Back.
Sleeves: Using finer needles and white, cast on 42 (50) sts and work 8 cm or 3" in K 2, P 2 rib. Change to thicker needles and st st and in R 1 increase in every 2nd and 3rd st alternately (every 3rd st) 16 times — 58 (66) sts. Now increase 1 st each end of every 10th R 9 times — 76 (84) sts. Work straight to 44 (45) cm or 17¼" (17¾").
Shape Top: At beginning of next 2 R cast off 4 (6) sts. Leave remaining 68 (72) sts on st holders.
Yoke: Now using thicker circular needle, K across all sts, but K last st of each needle together with 1st st of next needle to form raglan seams (4 decreases in rnd) — 300 (316) sts. Continue in rnds, decreasing at raglan seams in every 2nd rnd thus: K to st before seam, slip this st and next st, and K following st, then pass slip sts over — 8 sts decreased in rnd. *At the same time*, mark the 1st (5th) yoke rnd for embroidery with colored strand. Continue decreasing as before until 40 (44) yoke rnds have been worked and 140 sts remain for each size, ending after a plain rnd — 43 sts on Back and Front and 27 sts on each Sleeve.
Front Neck Shaping: Keeping continuity of armhole decreases throughout, slip center 7 sts on safety pin and work back and forth on all sts, decreasing: At beginning of R cast off 3 sts 4 times, 2 sts 6 times — 1 st left at each half Front, 17 sts on each Sleeve, and 33 sts on Back. Now decrease at Back raglan seam as before and decrease 1 st at front edge at beginning of next 2 R — all Front sts decreased. Decreasing at Back raglan as before, at other sleeve edge, cast off 8 sts at beginning of next 2 R, then 2 sts 2 times, and 3 sts 2 times — all sleeve sts decreased and 25 Back sts remain. Leave on st holder.
Finishing: Press carefully. Work the embroidery. Begin at the center of each part on the marked R and work the pattern toward the sides. Then to right and left of the raglan sts make red crosses and embroider along the raglan seams, staggering the crosses in every 2nd R. Finally, work one R of crosses on 4th st st R at lower edge of Back, Front, and Sleeves. Join seams. Now using the finer circular

Scattering of snowflakes

Black and red motifs offer a strong contrast to the pure white background of this pullover. The raglan seams and the top of the bands are also picked out in cross-stitch.

▸ Half-pattern in small (large) size. The numbers are centimeters; inches are in the directions.

needle, K across the Back sts, then pick up and K 29 sts down to Front safety pin, K across sts, and pick up and K 29 sts to shoulder. Work in K 2, P 2 rib in rnds for 24 cm or 9½". Cast off loosely in rib.

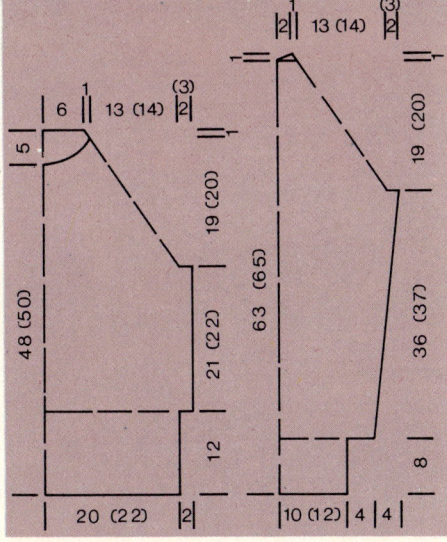

Embroidery Chart: 1 repeat of the yoke pattern is shown: Every x = 1 cross-stitch, 1 st wide and 1 R high, in the color shown.

Size: Directions are for 88 cm or 34½" bust. Changes for 96 cm or 37½" bust are in brackets.

Materials Required:

270 (300) gm or 9 (11) oz light blue, 90 (120) gm or 4 (5) oz red, 30 gm or 2 oz each in navy and white. Knitting needles and circular needles sizes 2 and 1 (Am) or 11 and 12 (Eng). St holders.

Basic Stitch: St st.

Color Sequence: *2 R each red, navy, and red, 6 R of Knitting Chart*, 2 R each red, navy and red.

Knitting Chart: 4 sts and 6 R form a complete pattern. Repeat the 4 sts across R; end as shown on Chart, keeping an edge st each end.

Tension: 28 sts and 40 R = 10 cm or 4".

Abbreviations: K = knit. P = purl. St(s) = stitch(es). R = row(s). Rnd(s) = round(s). St st = stocking or stockinette stitch.

DIRECTIONS

Back: Using finer needles and light blue, cast on 128 (140) sts and work 10 cm or 4" in K 1, P 1 rib. Change to thicker needles and work in st st following Color Sequence, working 1st R of Knitting Chart thus: K 1 (edge st), repeat the 4 sts 31 (34) times, K 2 from end of chart, then K 1 for edge st. Change to light blue and work straight to 31 cm or 12¼".

Shape Armholes: Place 22 sts each end on st holders and work on remaining 84 (96) sts, working from * to * of Color Sequence 2 times, then work the 6 R of stripes 1 time. Continue in light blue to 53 (54) cm or 20¾" (21¼").

Shape Neck: Cast off center 38 (44) sts and work on each side separately. At beginning of every 2nd R at neck edge, cast off 2 sts 2 times and 1 st 2 times. Cast off 17 (20) sts in next armhole edge R.

Front: Work as for Back to 31 cm or 12¼", then slip the 22 sts on st holders. Work Color Sequence to match Back, dividing at center for opening and working each 42 (48) sts separately. At neck edge, in every 2nd R cast off 2 sts 2 (3) times, 1 st 12 (13) times, 1 st in every 4th R 7 times, then 1 st in every 6th R 2 times. Work straight until armhole measures same as Back to shoulder.

Cast off 17 (20) sts at armhole edge.

Sleeves: Using red and finer needles, cast on 58 (62) sts and work 10 cm or 4" in K 1, P 1 rib. In next R, P 4 (6), P twice into every st to last 4 (6) sts, P to end — 108 (112) sts. Change to thicker needles and work in Color Sequence 1 time, then continue in light blue to 60 cm or 23½". Cast off.

Neckband: Using red and finer circular needle, cast on 236 (240) sts. Mark the 2 center sts; work 4 cm or 1½" in K 1, P 1 rib, decreasing in every rnd by working to st before center sts, slip st and 1st center st on to right hand needle, K next st and pass the 2 slipped sts over. Cast off in rib at 4 cm or 1½".

Finishing: Join shoulder seams. Using the thicker circular needle and red, K across sts on st holders, picking up 144 (150) sts along armhole edge in between. Mark the 22nd st from each edge for corner shaping. Work in st st, decreasing on next 2 rnds as for V-neck shaping of Neckband, K 1 rnd, then repeat these 3 rnds for 4 cm or 1½". Cast off. Join sleeve seam and sew to armhole band. Sew on Neckband. Press seams.

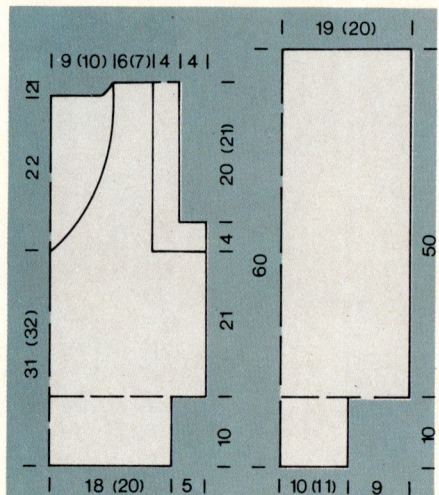

▲ **Half-pattern for small (large) size.** The numbers are centimeters; inches are in the directions.

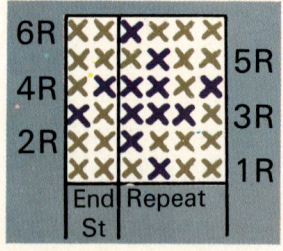

◀ **Knitting Chart:** Chart shows 1 repeat and end sts. Blue x = 1 navy st. Grey x = 1 white st.

▶ Here you see the added armhole band joining the sleeve to the pullover.

2326

Pull-on plus

With masculine appeal

Knitting

Here is a classic sweater with a difference. Knitted in pure wool for warmth, the sleeves and back are worked in a plain color in stocking or stockinette stitch while the front is patterned in an unusual two-color design.

FOR BOTH

Size: Directions are for 100 cm or 39½" chest. Changes for 112 cm or 44" chest are in brackets.

Materials Required:

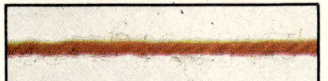

[100 gm = 300 m or 327 yds]. Green Pullover: 300 (350) gm or 11 (13) oz dark green, 200 (250) gm or 8 (9) oz light green. Blue Pullover: 400 (450) gm or 15 (16) oz navy, 100 gm or 4 oz light blue, 50 gm or 2 oz red. Knitting needles and a circular needle size 2 (Am) or 11 (Eng). St holder.

Basic Pattern 1: St st.

Basic Pattern 2: Use circular needle, but work back and forth. R 1: (wrong side) With light blue or light green, P. R 2: (wrong side) With navy or dark green, P. R 3: (right side) With navy or dark green, K. R 4: (right side) With light blue or light green, K 1, *K 3, then K 1 inserting needle 2 R down, repeat from * ending R K 4. R 5: (wrong side) With navy or dark green, P. R 6: (right side) With navy or dark green, K. R 7: (wrong side) With light blue or light green, K 1, *P 1 inserting needle 2 R down, P 3, repeat from * ending P 2, K 1 instead of P 3. R 8: (wrong side) With navy or dark green, P. R 9: (right side) With navy or dark green, K. R 10: (right side) With light blue or light green, K 1, *K 1, K 1 inserting 2 R down, K 2, repeat from * to end. R 11: (wrong side) With navy or dark green, P. R 12: (right side) With navy or dark green, K. R 13: (wrong side) With light blue or light green, K 1, *P 2, P 1 inserting 2 R down, P 1, repeat from * ending K 1 instead of P 1. Repeat R 2–13. (See How-to, right.)

Tension: 24 sts and 34 R = 10 cm or 4".

Abbreviations: K = knit. P = purl. St(s) = stitch(es). R = row(s). Rnd(s) = round(s). St st = stocking or stockinette stitch.

BLUE PULLOVER

Back: Using red and knitting needles, cast on 125 (137) sts and work in K 1, P 1 rib, working 2 R red, 3 R light blue, 3 R red, 12 R navy, 3 R red, 3 R light blue. Change to Basic Pattern 1 and work straight to 40 cm or 15¾".

Shape Armholes: At beginning of every R, cast off 5 sts 2 times, 3 sts 2 times,

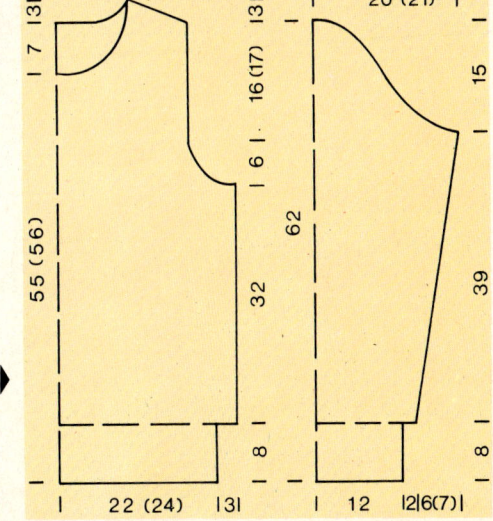

Here is a variation of the basic design. This is worked completely in the two-color pattern with plain borders.

Half-pattern for small (large) size. The numbers are centimeters; inches are given in the directions.

2 sts 6 times, 1 st 2 times, then 1 st each end of every 4th R 2 times — 91 (103) sts. Work straight to 62 (63) cm or 24¼" (24¾"). Shape Neck and Shoulders: Cast off center 29 sts and work on each side separately. At neck edge, in every 2nd R cast off 3 sts 3 times and 2 sts 1 time. *At the same time,* at armhole edge, in every 2nd R cast off 4 (6) sts 1 time and 4 (5) sts 4 times.

Front: Work border as for Back, then change to Basic Pattern 2, shaping as for Back to 55 (56) cm or 21½" (22").

Shape Neck: Cast off center 11 sts and work on each side separately. At neck edge, in every 2nd R cast off 3 sts 1 time, 2 sts 3 times, and 1 st 11 times. *At the same time,* at 62 (63) cm or 24¼" (24¾") shape shoulder as for Back.

Sleeves: Using red and knitting needles, cast on 73 sts and work in K 1, P 1 rib in colors as for Back border. Work in Basic Pattern 1 and increase 1 st each end of every 9th (8th) R 10 (7) times, then 1 st every 10th (7th) R 4 (11) times — 101 (109) sts. Work straight to 47 cm or 18½".

Shape Top: At beginning of every R, cast off 5 (6) sts 2 times, 3 (4) sts 4 times, 2 sts 6 times, 1 st 10 times, then 1 st each end of every 4th R 3 times. At beginning of every R, cast off 1 st 6 times, 2 sts 6 times, 3 sts 4 times, 5 sts 2 times — 11 (13) sts. Cast off.

Finishing: Join all seams. Using circular needle, pick up and K 128 sts around neck. Work 9 rnds navy, 3 rnds red, 3 rnds light blue, 3 rnds red. Cast off.

GREEN PULLOVER

Work as for Blue Pullover, but work all ribbed borders in dark green and Back, Front, and Sleeves in light and dark green.

Staggered pattern

How-to

Work back and forth with circular needle in open rows, beginning each row at the edge where the required colored thread hangs. With the main color P a row on the wrong side, then K a row on the right side.

In the contrast color, K 1 row on right side in the following way: *K 3, K 1 inserting needle into st 2 rows down, repeat from *.

When you work into a st 2 rows down, the freed st of the main color is unravelled and the st of the contrast color covers the two horizontal threads.

Work 2 more st st rows in the main color, then work a P row in the contrast color in which every 4th P st is worked into the st 2 rows down.

Knitting

Made for him

A discriminating man will love this pullover with matching socks. The diamond pattern is worked in a band around the pullover and socks, and then outlined with Swiss darning or duplicate stitch.

MAN'S PULLOVER

Size: Directions are for 96 cm or 38" chest. Changes for 102 cm or 40" chest are in brackets.

Materials Required:

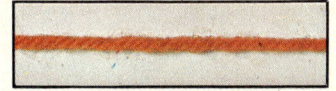

450 (500) gm or 16 (18) oz in main color, 50 gm or 2 oz each in medium blue and white [50 gm = 210 m or 230 yds]. Knitting needles sizes 1 and 2 (Am) or 11 and 12 (Eng). Circular needle size 1 (Am) or 12 (Eng). Stitch holder.

Basic Stitch: Stocking or stockinette stitch.

Knitting Chart: Each color sign = 1 st in colors given in the directions. The red crosses are worked in the same color as the other sts in that area. These sts are later embroidered in Swiss darning or duplicate st. 32 sts form one repeat. For 1st R, work edge st, then begin at 26th (20th) st and work to end, then work from 1st–32nd sts 4 times, finally 1st–8th st again and K edge st. Work R 1–17 as given, then work in reverse from R 1–16.

Tension: 29 sts and 40 R = 10 cm or 4".

Abbreviations: K = knit. P = purl. St(s) = stitch(es). R = row(s). Rnd(s) = round(s). St st = stocking or stockinette st.

2331

Knitting

DIRECTIONS

Back: Using main color and finer needles, cast on 145 (157) sts and work 12 cm or $4\frac{3}{4}"$ in K 1, P 1 rib. Change to thicker needles and work in Basic Stitch, following Knitting Chart for 33 rows, working the blue crosses in white and the grey crosses in medium blue for R 1–16 and in main color for 2nd half of the design. The red crosses are worked in the same color as the other sts in that area and then later worked in Swiss darning or duplicate st. Continue in main color in st st to 40 cm or $15\frac{3}{4}"$.

Shape Armholes: At beginning of every R, cast off 4 (5) sts 2 times, 3 (4) sts 2 times, 2 sts 6 times, 1 st 8 (10) times – 111 (117) sts. Work straight to 62 (63) cm or $24\frac{3}{8}"$ ($24\frac{3}{4}"$).

Shape Neck and Shoulders: Cast off center 47 sts and work on each side separately. At neck edge, in every 2nd R cast off 2 sts 2 times and 1 st 1 time. *At the same time,* at armhole edge, in every 2nd R cast off 4 (5) sts 3 times and 5 (5) sts 3 times.

Front: Work as for Back to 40 cm or $15\frac{3}{4}"$.

Shape Neck and Armholes: Leave center st on safety pin; divide work and work on each side separately. Work armhole and shoulder shapings as for Back. *At the same time,* at neck edge, decrease 1 st on next R 10 times, then 1 st in every 2nd R 5 times, every 4th R 7 times, and every 6th R 6 times.

Sleeves: Using main color and finer needles, cast on 80 sts and work 10 cm or 4" in K 1, P 1 rib. Change to thicker needles and work in st st, increasing 1 st each end of every 8th (7th) R 17 (20) times – 114 (120) sts. Work straight to 48 cm or 19".

Shape Top: At beginning of every R, cast off 5 (6) sts 2 times, 4 (5) sts 2 times, 3 sts 4 times, 2 sts 4 times, 1 st 6 times, 1 st each end of every 4th R 6 times. At beginning of every R, cast off 1 st 6 times, 2 sts 4 times, 3 sts 4 times, 4 (5) sts 2 times, and 5 (6) sts 2 times. Cast off remaining 14 (12) sts.

Finishing: Embroider the diamond pattern in Swiss darning or duplicate stitch where marked in red. Work in medium blue on main color and white and main color on medium blue. Press work on wrong side. Join all seams. Using circular needle and main color, pick up and K 224 sts all around neck edge, including center st on safety pin. Work in rnds of K 1, P 1 rib and work 1st rnd to 1 st before center, then slip 1, K 2 together, pass slip st over, work in rib to end. Work in rib for 2 cm or $\frac{3}{4}"$, decreasing 2 sts at center on every rnd. Change to medium blue and work 2 cm or $\frac{3}{4}"$, still decreasing as before. Cast off in rib. Press seams.

SOCKS

Size: Shoe size 9–$9\frac{1}{2}$ (Am) or $7\frac{1}{2}$–8 (Eng). Length can be adjusted to fit other sizes.

Materials Required: Yarn (see sample for Pullover): 100 gm or 4 oz in main color, 50 gm in contrasting color. Remnants of a third color for embroidery. Knitting needles sizes 1 and 2 (Am) or 11 and 12 (Eng). 5 double-pointed needles size 2 (Am) or 11 (Eng).

Basic Stitch: Stocking or stockinette stitch.

Knitting Chart: Same as for Man's Pullover, but work from 1st–32nd st 2 times, with 1 st each end as edge st. Use a separate ball of yarn for each color area, twisting the strands at changeover to avoid a hole. Do not carry yarn across back, as this will tighten the work.

Tension and Abbreviations: See Man's Pullover.

DIRECTIONS

Using main color and finer needles, cast on 66 sts and work 7 cm or $2\frac{3}{4}"$ in K 1, P 1 rib. Change to thicker needles and work in Basic Pattern to 13 cm or 5". Now work from the Knitting Chart, working grey crosses in main color and blue crosses in contrasting color. Red crosses are worked in same color as other sts in that area. These are later embroidered in Swiss darning or duplicate st. When the 33 rows are completed, cast off 1 st each end of next R. With double-pointed needles, placing 16 sts on each of 4 needles, and with 5th needle continue in main color for 2 rnds. Now leave the 2nd and 3rd needles unworked and work for 30 R on the 1st and 4th needles for heel.

Shape Heel: K across 21 sts, then K 2 together through back of sts, turn, slip first st, P to last 11 sts, P 2 together through back of sts, turn, slip first st, K to last 10 sts, K 2 together through back of sts, turn, slip first st, P to last 10 sts, P 2 together, turn. Continue decreasing in this way until only the 12 center sts remain, ending after a P R. Break off yarn. Now K across 15 slipped sts, K center 12 sts, K across 15 slipped sts at other side of heel. K across 2nd and 3rd needles. Arrange the 42 heel sts on the 1st and 4th needles evenly and continue for 2 rnds. In next rnd, K to last 3 sts of 1st needle, K 2 together, K 1, K across 2nd and 3rd needles. On 4th needle K 1, K 2 together through back of sts, K to end of needle. Work 2 rnds. Repeat these 3 rnds 4 times more – 64 sts. Work straight until foot measures 23 cm or 9" (or length required), measured from beginning of heel decreases.

Shape for Toe: In next rnd, K to last 3 sts of 1st needle, K 2 together, K 1. On 2nd needle, K 1, K 2 together through back of sts, K to end. Work 3rd and 4th needles as 1st and 2nd needle. Repeat this decrease on every 2nd rnd 5 times more, then on every rnd 8 times more. Draw thread tightly through remaining 8 sts and fasten off.

Finishing: Embroider diamond in Swiss darning or duplicate st, then sew up back seam. Press.

Above are shown several color variations for the socks. Choose a striking color contrast or blending tones for the diamond design.

Knitting Chart: R 1–17 and sts 1–32 form 1 repeat pattern. Each color sign = 1 st. See the directions for colors. The red crosses indicate the embroidered outlines.

Half-pattern for small (large) size. The numbers are in centimeters; the inches are in the directions.

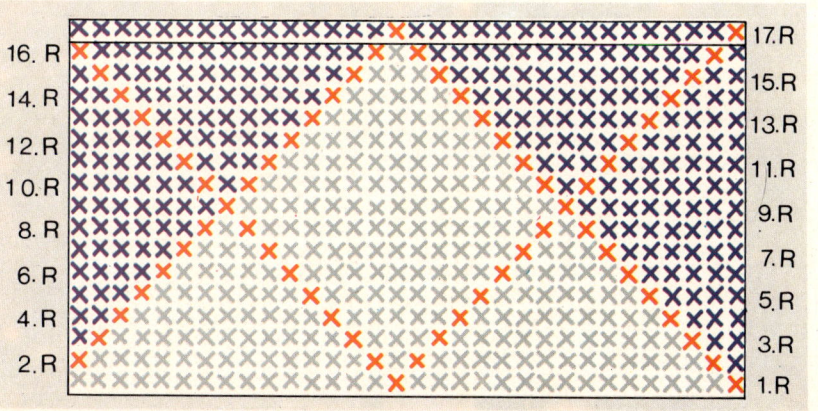
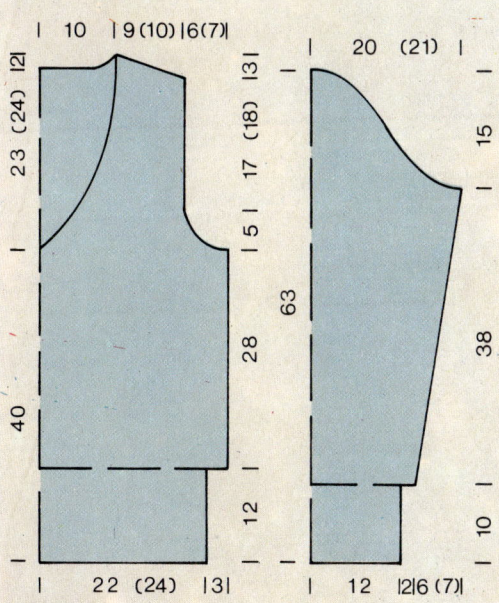

2333

This two-tone tank top is more difficult and will take longer to knit because the stitches have to be crossed in the wrong side rows.

Knitting

Good connections

Here are two versions of a tank top which will delight expert knitters. It can be made in one or two colors as shown on the left. The fronts are worked in a diamond pattern; the backs are worked in the main color in stocking or stockinette stitch.

Size: Directions are for 96 cm or 37½″ chest. Changes for 104 cm or 41″ chest are in brackets.

Materials Required:

[50 gm = 114 m or 124 yds]. **Striped Pullover:** 350 (400) gm or 13 (15) oz in brown, 50 gm or 2 oz beige. **Plain Pullover:** 400 (450) gm or 15 (16) oz rust. Knitting needles and circular needle size 5 (Am) or 8 (Eng).

Basic Pattern 1: St st.
Basic Pattern 2: Follow the Knitting Chart. 14 sts and 28 R form one complete diamond. Repeat the pattern as instructed. **Striped Pullover:** Work back and forth on the circular needle, always beginning where relevant colored yarn is hanging, thus working 2 rows on right side, then 2 rows on wrong side. After brown border, work 1st R of Knitting Chart using beige. Even-numbered R are worked in st st on all sts. **Plain Pullover:** P all wrong side R.

Tension 1: 22 sts over st st = 10 cm or 4″.
Tension 2: 24 sts over pattern = 10 cm or 4″.

Abbreviations: K = knit. P = purl. St(s) = stitch(es). R = row(s). Rnd(s) = round(s). St st = stocking or stockinette st.

Though only one color is used, the diamond pattern lends an interesting texture to the fabric.

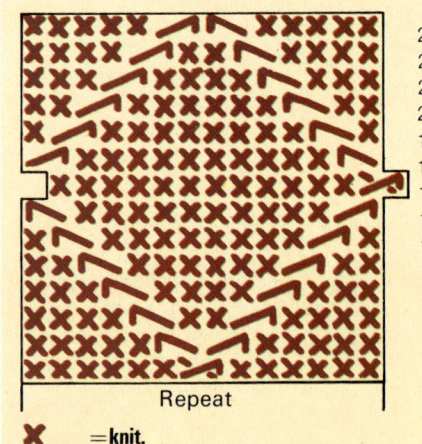

◀ **Knitting Chart:** Only the right side rows are shown, purl all wrong side rows. Rows 1–28 form 1 repeat.

Half-pattern for small (large) size. The numbers are centimeters; inches are given in the directions. ▶

✕ = knit.
= slip st to right.
= slip st to left.
= cross 2 slip stitches to right.

DIRECTIONS

Back: Using brown or rust, cast on 110 (120) sts and work 12 cm or 4¾" in K 2, P 2 rib. Continue in Basic Pattern 1 to 36 cm or 14¼".
Shape Armholes: At beginning of every R cast off 6 (8) sts 2 times, 3 sts 2 times, 2 sts 4 times, 1 st 6 times, then decrease 1 st each end of every 4th R 2 times — 74 (80) sts. Work straight to 57 (58) cm or 22½" (22¾").
Shape Neck and Shoulders: Cast off center 32 sts and work on each side separately. At neck edge, in every 2nd R cast off 2 sts 2 times and 1 st 2 times. *At the same time,* at 58 (59) cm or 22¾" (23¼") at armhole edge, in every 2nd R cast off 5 (6) sts 3 times.
Front: Using brown or rust, cast on 120 (130) sts and work 12 cm or 4¾" in K 2, P 2 rib. **Note:** Use circular needle for Striped Pullover. P next R in main color. Continue in Basic Pattern 2, working 1st R thus: K 1 (edge st), then work from 12th (14th) st of Knitting Chart, repeat 1st–14th sts 8 (9) times, then 1st–3rd sts (1st st only) and end with 1 edge st. Continue in Basic Pattern 2 to 33 cm or 13", keeping edge st each end.
Shape Neck: Divide work at center and work on each side separately. At neck edge, in every 2nd R cast off 2 sts 2 times, 1 st 9 times, then 1 st every 4th R 6 times and 1 st every 6th R 5 times. *At the same time,* when piece measures 36 cm or 14¼", shape armholes in every 2nd R at armhole edge by casting off 6 (8) sts 1 time, 3 sts 1 (2) times, 2 sts 2 (1) times, and 1 st 6 times. Work straight at armhole edge, still decreasing at neck edge as given until shaping is completed — 74 (80) sts. Work straight to 58 (59) cm or 22¼" (23¼"), ending at armhole edge.
Shape Shoulder: At beginning of every 2nd R at armhole edge, cast off 5 (6) sts 1 (2) times and 6 (7) sts 2 (1) times.
Neckband: Using circular needle and brown or rust, cast on 204 sts and work in rnds of K 2, P 2 rib. Mark center 2 sts and decrease 1 st each side of these 2 sts on every 2nd rnd 6 times. Work 4 rnds straight then increase 1 st each side of the center 2 sts on every 2nd rnd 6 times. Cast off in rib.
Armhole Bands: Using brown or rust and circular needle, cast on 120 sts and work in rnds of K 2, P 2 rib for 8 cm or 3¼". Cast off in rib.
Finishing: Join all seams. Sew on neck and armhole bands. Fold in half to inside and stitch down.

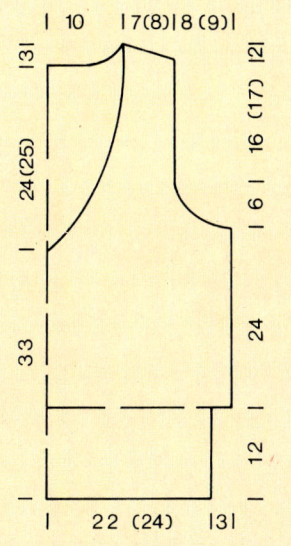

How-to

Diamond pattern

1 Crossing slip stitch to right: Working in 1 or 2 colors, K to st before slip st. Insert needle into slip st from right to left and draw it to the right in front of 1st st, K the 1st st, and slip both off the left needle.

2 Crossing slip stitch to left: K to the slip st. Insert needle behind slip st and into the front of the next st, K this st, insert needle into slip st from right to left and slip both sts off left needle.

3 Crossing to the left from the wrong side (for two-color pattern): P to st before slip st, skip next st, insert needle into back of slip st from right to left, slip both sts off, replace skipped st on left needle and P.

4 Crossing to right from the wrong side: P to slip st. Skip slip st, P next st but do not slip from needle, insert needle into slip st, and slip both sts off left needle.

The classic view

BOTH STYLES

Size: Directions are for 100 cm or 39½" chest. Changes for 108 cm or 42½" chest are in brackets.

Materials Required:

600 (650) gm or 22 (23) oz beige or rust [50 gm = 150 m or 165 yds]. Knitting needles sizes 2 and 4 (Am) or 9 and 11 (Eng). Circular needle size 2 (Am) or 11 (Eng).

Basic Stitch 1: See Knitting Chart. One repeat of pattern is given. P all wrong side R. Work the crossing st thus: with the right needle, pass behind the 1st st and K into the 2nd st knitwise, then K into the 1st st, yarn over needle, slip 2nd st on right-hand needle over 1st st and yarn-over st.

Basic Stitch 2: St st.

Tension 1 and 2: 26 sts and 36 R = 10 cm or 4".

Abbreviations: K = knit. P = purl. St(s) = stitch(es). St st = stocking or stockinette st. R = row(s). Rnd(s) = round(s).

DIRECTIONS

Back: Using finer needles, cast on 134 (144) sts and work 10 cm or 4" in K 1, P 1 rib. Change to thicker needles and work in Basic Stitch 1, following Chart A for Beige Pullover and Chart B for Rust Pullover. Work R 1 thus: K 1 (edge st), repeat sts 1–10 13 (14) times, sts 11–12 1 time, K 1 (edge st). Work straight in pattern to 40 cm or 15¾".

Shape Armholes: At beginning of every R, cast off 3 sts 4 times, 2 sts 6 times, and 1 st 8 times – 102 (112) sts. Work straight to 56 (57) cm or 22 (22½)".

Shape Shoulders: At beginning of every R, cast off 5 sts 4 (14) times and 4 sts 14 (4) times. Leave remaining 26 sts on spare needle.

Right Sleeve: Using finer needles, cast on 68 sts and work 8 cm or 3" in K 1, P 1 rib. Change to thicker needles and st st and increase 1 st each end of every 8th R 16 times (alternately every 6th and 8th R, 18 times) – 100 (104) sts. Work straight to 48 cm or 19".

Shape Top: At beginning of every R, cast off 3 (4) sts 2 times, 2 sts 8 times, 1 st 28 times, 2 sts 8 times, 3 sts 2 times, 3 (4) sts 2 times. Work straight on remaining 22 sts for 13 (14) cm or 5" (5½")**, ending after a P row. Cast off 5 sts at beginning of next R and on every 2nd R at same edge, cast off 5 sts 1 time and 4 sts 3 times.

Left Sleeve: Work to match Right Sleeve to **, ending after a K R. Work as for Right Sleeve to end.

BEIGE PULLOVER

Front: Work as for Back to 54 (55) cm or 21¼" (21¾").

Shape Neck and Shoulders: Cast off center 10 sts and work on each side separately. At neck edge, in every 2nd R cast off 3 sts 2 times, 2 sts 2 times, and 1 st 6 times. *At the same time*, at 56 (57) cm or 22" (22½"), shape shoulder by casting off 5 sts 2 times and 4 (5) sts 5 times.

Finishing: Join seams, sewing extension of Sleeves between Front and Back. Now using circular needle, pick up and K 62 sts around Front Neck, 20 sts along top of each Sleeve, and K across 26 Back neck sts. Work in rnds of K 1, P 1 rib for 4 cm or 1½". Cast off.

RUST PULLOVER

Front: Work as for Back to 43 (44) cm or 17" (17¼").

Shape for Neck: Divide work at center and work on each side separately, keeping

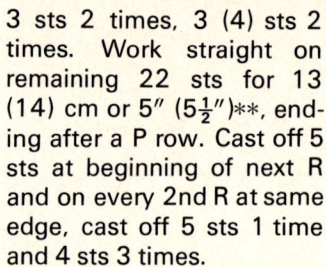

The beige pullover has a vertical zigzag pattern and a crew neck.

The zigzag pattern on the V-neck pullover runs in horizontal lines. Sleeves and shoulder yoke are plain in both styles.

continuity of armhole decreases. At neck edge, in every 2nd R decrease 1 st 13 times, then 1 st every 4th R 6 times, 1 st every 6th R 2 times. *At the same time*, shape shoulder at 56 (57) cm or 22" (22½") as for Beige Pullover.

Finishing: Sew up as for Beige Pullover. Using the circular needle, K across Back sts, pick up and K 20 sts from top of each Sleeve, 52 sts down each Front and 1 st from center Front. Work in rnds of K 1, P 1 rib, working each rnd to 1 st before center st, slip 1, K 2 together, pass slip stitch over, rib to end of rnd. Work thus to 4 cm or 1½". Cast off loosely in rib.

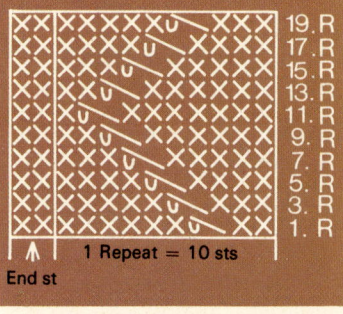

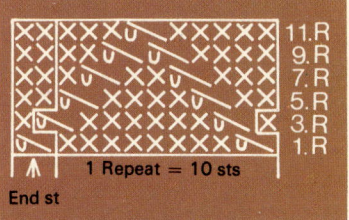

Knitting Charts: 1 repeat of each pattern is given.
X = 1 knit stitch
U = 1 crossing stitch with yarn over (see directions)

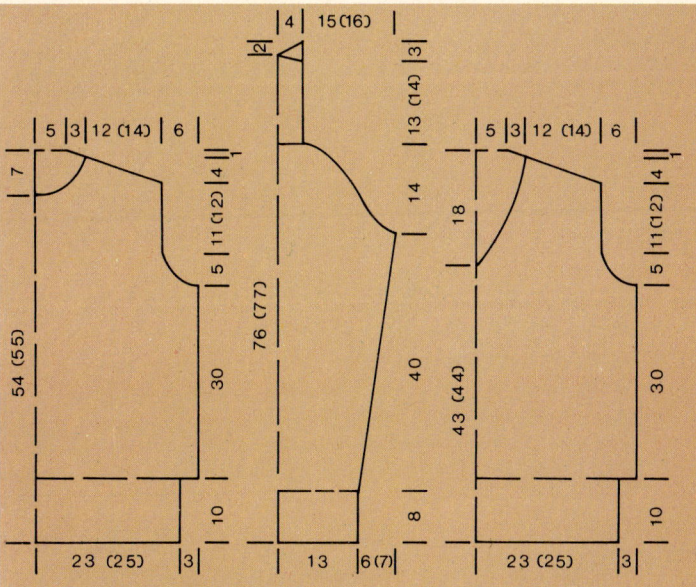

Half-pattern for Beige Pullover (left), sleeve (center), and Rust Pullover (right). The numbers are centimeters; inches are in the directions.

2337

Snow white

A delicate lacy mat will show off your crochet skills. The snowflake design is created with single and double crochet, so it's not as difficult to work as it looks.

Size: 28 cm or 11" square.
Materials Required:

Cotton: 50 gm or 2 oz white. Crochet hook size 1.

Abbreviations: Ch = chain. Sc = single crochet. Dc = double crochet. R = row(s). St(s) = stitch(es). Rnd(s) = round(s).

Center Cross: (make 4 strips) Make 18 ch, turn and work R 1 in the 2nd st from hook. R 1: (right side) 1 sc in each of 8 ch, 3 sc in the 9th st, 1 sc in each of last 8 ch. R 2: Turn without ch sts and, beginning in the 2nd st, work in sc in the back threads of previous R, again working 3 sc in the center of the 3 sc sts. Repeat R 2 until 29 R in all have been worked. Fasten off.
Sew the 4 strips together at points.
Round Motif: Make 10 ch and join in a ring with a slip st, then 3 ch for 1st dc and 2 dc in ring, *1 picot (3 ch, 1 slip st into front thread of the dc below), then 3 dc in ring, repeat from * 10 times, 1 picot, close rnd with a slip st into 3rd of beginning ch. *At the same time,* join the motif onto the Center Cross while working picot after 1 ch by withdrawing the hook from the loop and drawing it through the st where it is to be attached. Make 2 ch and finish picot as before.

DIRECTIONS

Work the Center Cross then attach the Round Motifs. **Beginning at center of Cross, join the 1st Motif onto the sc of the 23rd R of the right strip with the 1st picot, then join the 4th picot onto the sc of the 23rd R of the left strip and continue to finish the Motif. Join the following 3 Motifs only onto the right strip thus: **2nd Motif:** 1st picot onto the 15th R, 4th picot onto the 10th picot of the 1st Motif. **3rd Motif:** 1st picot onto the 7th R, 4th picot onto the 10th picot of 2nd Motif. **4th Motif:** 1st picot onto the 1st R, 4th picot onto the 10th picot of 3rd Motif.
The 2nd R consists of 3 Motifs and is parallel to 1st R. Each Motif is joined with the 1st picot onto the 7th picot of the Motif in the previous R. Join the 4th picot of 1st Motif to the 15th R of left strip and 2nd and 3rd Motifs onto the 10th picot of the previous Motif. The 3rd R has 2 Motifs. The 1st picot of 1st Motif is worked onto the 7th picot of the 1st Motif of previous R, the 4th picot onto the 7th R of left strip. Join the 2nd Motif as in 2nd R. Join the single Motif with 1st picot onto 7th picot of adjoining Motif, and 4th picot to 1st R of strip. Repeat from ** 3 times more.
Corner Motifs: (make 4) After the 1st picot, make 7 ch, join to the 9th foundation st of the strip, 7 ch, 1 slip st in the back thread of the dc, finish picot. Join the 4th picot onto the 10th picot of the left Motif, the 10th picot onto the 7th picot of the right Motif. Work all corners to match.
Crochet Edging: *Into a loose outside-edge picot, work 1 dc, 1 picot, (working slip st of picot in sc below), 2 ch, repeat from * all around outer edges (see photograph). Fasten off. Starch and press.

Crochet

Charming, old-fashioned atmosphere

Crochet

COVER

Size: 180 cm x 235 cm or 72" x 93½".

Materials Required:

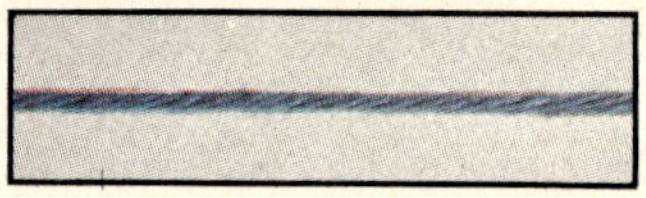

1600 gm or 57 oz white. Crochet hook size D.

Basic Pattern: Follow Crochet Diagram, repeating R 1–12. For odd-numbered rows, read diagram from right to left and for even-numbered rows read from left to right.

Tension: 26 sts and 12 R = 10 cm or 4".

Abbreviations: Ch = chain. St(s) = stitch(es). Dc = double crochet. R = row(s).

DIRECTIONS

Cover: Make 496 ch and follow the chart, working 1st dc into 3rd ch from hook, then follow diagram to end of R – 494 sts. The diagram consists of 82 sts which are repeated 6 times across R, with 1 extra edge st at each end. Work R 1–12 18 times in all. Fasten off.

Lace Edging: For the first edging, make 60 ch: follow and work in pattern as for diagram, working 1st dc into 3rd ch from hook, and working over the 58 sts to arrow showing end of first edging. *Keeping end of odd-numbered R straight, increase 2 sts at other edge on 2nd to 7th R, working extra sts into dc. Then, keeping continuity of pattern, decrease 2 sts on same edge on next 6 R. Continue thus until 18 repeats of pattern have been worked. Fasten off. Work second lace edging to match, working in reverse and beginning where arrow indicates on the diagram.

Finishing: Press well. Sew edgings across short ends.

CUSHION

Size: 38 cm or 15" in diameter.

Materials Required:

150 gm or 6 oz old rose. Crochet hook size E.

For the ruffles, several trebles are worked into the front of the stitches in that round.

Each short end is edged with a pointed lace pattern which is worked from the same crochet diagram below.

Crochet diagram: 82 stitches and 12 R form 1 repeat. For the odd-numbered rows, read the diagram from right to left; read even-numbered rows from left to right.

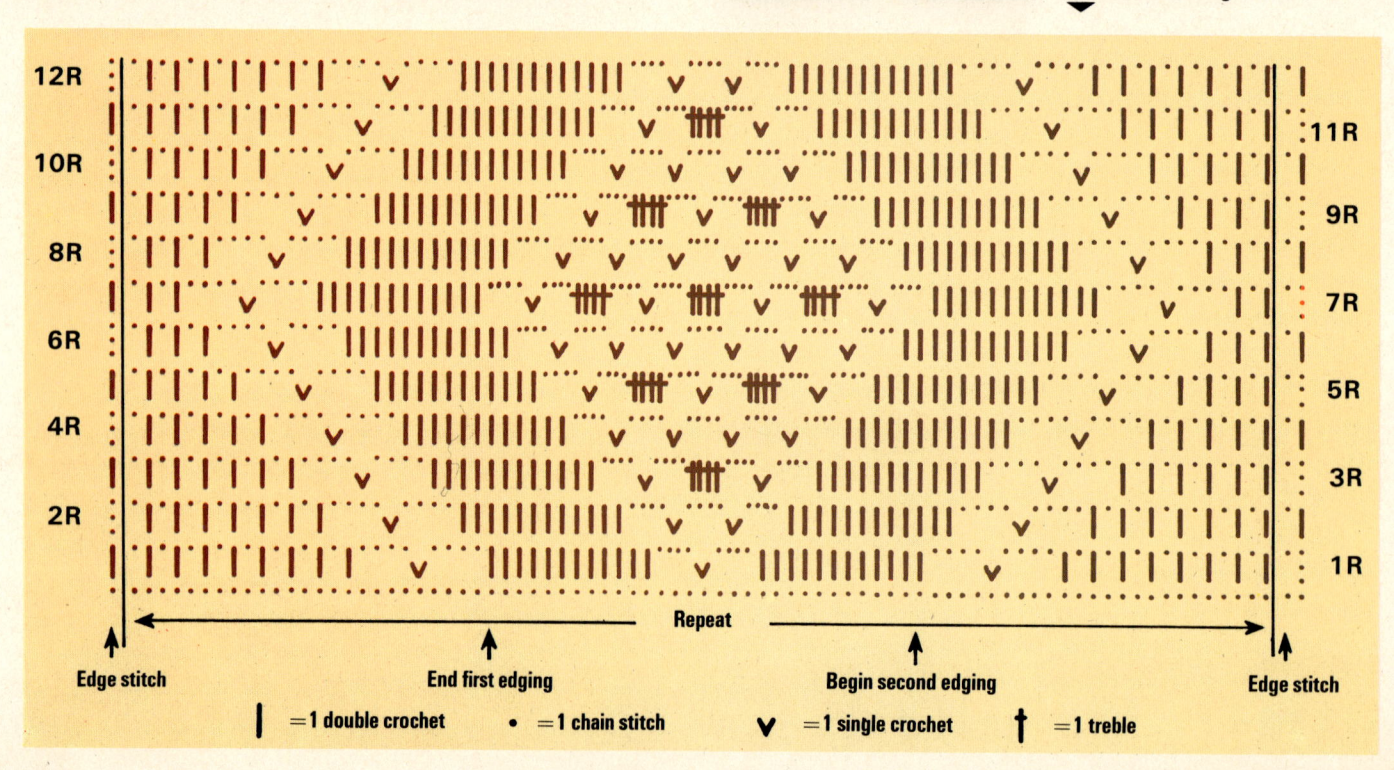

| = 1 double crochet   • = 1 chain stitch   v = 1 single crochet   † = 1 treble

2340

Basic Pattern: Dc and tr worked in rounds.
Tension: 20 sts and 9 R = 10 cm or 4".
Abbreviations: Ch = chain. St(s) = stitch(es). Dc = double crochet. Tr = treble. Rnd(s) = round(s).

DIRECTIONS
Front: Make 5 ch and join into a ring with a slip st.
Rnd 1: With 3 ch as 1st dc, work 14 dc into ring. Join all rounds with a slip st into the last st of 1st ch. **Rnd 2:** 4 ch for 1st tr. In this and all following tr rnds, work tr into the front loop of the previous rnd, 2 tr into 1st st, then 3 tr in each st. **Rnd 3:** Work behind the 2nd rnd into the back loop, *1 dc into 1 st, 2 dc into next st, repeat from * all around. **Rnd 4:** With 3 ch as 1st dc, work 2 dc into each dc. **Rnd 5:** Repeat the method of Rnd 2, working into the front loops of last rnd. With 4 ch as 1st tr, work * 2 tr in each of next 2 dc, 3 tr in next dc, repeat from * all around. **Rnd 6:** Repeat Rnd 3, working into back loops of Rnd 4. **Rnd 7:** With 3 ch as 1st dc, work dc on dc. **Rnd 8:** With 4 ch as 1st tr, work *2 tr into next 2 dc, 1 tr in next dc, repeat from * all around. **Rnd 9:** Repeat Rnd 7, working into the back loop of Rnd 7. **Rnd 10:** With 3 ch as 1st dc, work * 2 dc in each of next 2 dc, 1 dc in next dc, repeat from * all around. **Rnds 11–22:** Repeat Rnds 8–10 4 times. Fasten off.
Back: Make 5 ch, join into a ring with a slip st, and work in rounds of dc, increasing to match Front until the Back is the same diameter as the Front. Then fasten off the yarn.
Finishing: Press, then join Back and Front together from wrong side with single crochet, leaving opening for cushion. Turn to right side. Insert cushion. Sew the opening closed.

How-to

Crocheted ruffles

1 The circular ruffles of trebles are worked by crocheting into the front loops only of the previous double crochet round.

2 In the next round, fold the trebles toward you and work double crochet into the back loops of the last double crochet round.

3 In the following round, the double crochets are worked in the usual way, crocheting into both loops of the previous round.

4 When joining the front and back, place them right sides together and work a partial round of single crochet. Turn and insert cushion.

Creamy cobwebs

Size: 170 cm x 240 cm or 67" x 95".

Materials Required:

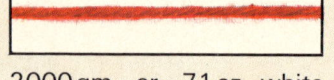

2000 gm or 71 oz white cotton. Crochet hook size D.

Basic Pattern: Motif: Make 6 ch and join into a ring with a slip st. Rnd 1: 2 ch, *1 small puff st by yarn around hook 3 times, insert hook into ring, draw up a loop, then yarn over and draw through 6 loops, yarn over and draw through remaining 2 loops, repeat from * 5 times more. Join this rnd and Rnds 2 and 3 with a slip st into top ch at beginning of rnd. Rnd 2: 3 ch as 1st dc, * then 3 ch, 1 dc in between the next 2 clusters, repeat from * 4 times more, 3 ch. Rnd 3: 2 ch, *1 large puff st by yarn over hook 5 times, insert hook into ch space of previous rnd, draw up a loop, yarn over and draw through 10 loops, yarn over and draw through 2 loops, 3 ch, 1 large puff st into same ch space, 3 ch, repeat from * 5 times more. Rnd 4: *3 ch, 1 sc in between the next 2 puff sts inserting hook around the ch loops of Rnds 2 and 3, 3 ch, then 1 sc into the next dc of Rnd 2 inserting hook round the ch loop of Rnd 3, repeat from * ending 1 slip st into 1st ch.
In Rnds 5–10, always work 3 ch as 1st dc. Rnd 5: 5 dc in 1st ch loop, *3 ch, skip 1 ch loop, 5 dc in next loop, repeat from * ending 3 ch, join with a slip st. Rnd 6: 2 dc, 3 dc in next dc, 2 dc, 2 ch, repeat from * all around, join with a slip st. Rnd 7: *2 dc, 3 dc in next dc, 1 dc, 3 dc in next dc, 2 dc, 2 ch, repeat from * all around, join with a slip st. Rnd 8: *3 dc, 3 dc in next dc, 3 dc, 3 dc in next dc, 3 dc, 2 ch, repeat from * all around, join with a slip st. Rnd 9:

Here you see in close-up the creamy texture of the hexagonal pattern, with puff stitches at the center of the flower.

*15 dc, 2 ch, repeat from * all around, join with a slip st. **Rnd 10:** 1 dc, 1 half-worked dc in next 2 sts and loop off together, 9 dc, 1 half-worked dc in next 2 sts and loop of together, 1 dc, *5 ch, 1 dc, 2 half-worked dc as before, 9 dc, 2 half-worked dc, 1 dc, repeat from * all around, 5 ch, join with a slip st. **Rnd 11:** *1 sc into 2nd st of group, 1 hdc, 8 dc, 1 hdc, 1 sc, 3 ch, 1 dc into 3rd of 5 ch, 3 ch, repeat from *, join with a slip st to sc. **Rnd 12:** Slip-st over the first 6 sts, *9 ch, 1 dc into 1st ch-loop, 3 ch, 1 dc into 2nd ch-loop, 9 ch, 1 slip st into the 6th and 7th sts, repeat from * ending last repeat of round with slip st into the 6th slip st. **Rnd 13:** *9 ch, 1 dc into the 8th of 9-ch loop, 3 ch, 1 dc into the 2nd ch of the small ch-loop, 3 ch, 1 dc into the 2nd ch of large ch-loop, 9 ch, 1 sc in between the 2 slip sts, repeat from * all around, join with a slip st. **Rnd 14:** *11 ch, 1 dc into the 2nd ch of 1st small ch-loop, 5 ch, 1 dc into the 2nd ch of next ch-loop, 11 ch, 1 sc in sc, repeat from * all around, join with a slip st and fasten off. These 14 rnds make one complete motif.

Tension: Each motif measures about 22 cm or $8\frac{1}{2}$".

Abbreviations: Ch = chain. Sc = single crochet. Dc = double crochet. Hdc = half dc. Rnd(s) = round(s).

DIRECTIONS
Make 95 motifs as given in Basic Pattern.
Finishing: Pin out motifs and steam-press lightly. *Join 1 row of 11 motifs together neatly, then in between them on next row join 10 motifs joining the 2 rows together. Repeat from * 3 times more, then add a final row of 11 motifs. Cut lengths of cotton yarn about 26 cm or $10\frac{1}{4}$" long. Knot into point and joins of outer motifs.

For a land of dreams

Crochet

Note: The directions are given for a single bed size which is three squares wide and five squares long.

✱

Size: 150 cm x 250 cm or 59" x 98" (excluding lace edging).
Materials Required:

3100 gm or 110 oz white [50 gm = 133 m or 145 yds]. Crochet hook size D.
Abbreviations: Ch = chain. Sc = single crochet. Dc = double crochet. Tr = treble. Cl = cluster. Sl st = slip stitch. R = row(s). Rnd(s) = round(s).

DIRECTIONS

The Square (15 required): Make 6 ch and join into a ring with a sl st. Rnd 1: With 3 ch as 1st dc, work 16 dc in ring. Rnd 2: With 1 ch as 1st sc, work in sc, working 2 sc into every 2nd dc — 24 sts. Rnd 3: Dc, working 2 dc into every 3rd sc — 32 sts. Rnd 4: *1 sc, 1 cl in next st (cl = 5 dc into next st, leaving last loop of each dc on hook, yarn over and draw through all loops, 1 ch), 1 sc, 2 sc in next st, repeat from * 7 times. Rnd 5: Dc, but at cl, work 2 dc into loop and ch. Rnd 6: Sc, working 2 sc into every 6th st — 56 sts. Rnd 7: With 4 ch as tr, work * 3 tr into 1st st, skip next st, then 2 dc, 2 half dc, 2 sc, 2 half dc, 2 dc, skip 1 st, 3 tr, 2 ch (corner), repeat from * 3 times more. Rnd 8: Sc, working 5 sc into each 2-ch loop at corner. Rnd 9: *1 dc, 1 ch, skip 1 st, repeat from * all around but working 1 dc, 1 ch, 1 dc, 1 ch, 1 dc into center sc at corner. Rnd 10: Sc, working 3 sc into corner dc. Rnd 11: Dc, working 5 dc into corner sc. Rnds 12 and 13: Repeat Rnds 10 and 11 — 148 sts.
In the following rnds, only sts between corners are given. At the corners, alternately work 3 sc or 3 dc. Rnd 14: 19 sc, 1 cl, 19 sc. Rnd 15: Dc, but above each cluster, leave last loop of the 2 dc on hook, yarn over, and draw through sts. Rnd 16: 19 sc, 1 cl, 5 sc, 1 cl, 19 sc. Rnd 17 and all right side rnds to Rnd 27: Repeat Rnd 15. Rnd 18: 19 sc, (1 cl, 5 sc) 2 times, 1 cl, 19 sc. Rnd 20: 19 sc, (1 cl, 5 sc) 3 times, 1 cl, 19 sc. Rnd 22: 25 sc, cl as in Rnd 18, 25 sc. Rnd 24: 31 sc, cl as in Rnd 16, 31 sc. Rnd 26: 37 sc, 1 cl, 37 sc. Rnd 28: Sc. Rnd 29: Dc. Rnd 30 and all following wrong side rnds: Sc. Rnd 31: Repeat Rnd 9. Rnd 33: Dc. Rnds 35, 37, 39: Repeat Rnd 9. Rnd 41: Dc. Rnd 42: Sc, working 2 sc, 1 ch, 2 sc into corner st. Fasten off. When all squares are completed, sew together on

wrong side, 3 squares in width and 5 squares in length.
Work lace edging thus: Make 9 ch. R 1: 1 dc into 6th ch from hook, 2 dc in next ch, 2 ch, 2 dc in next ch, 1 dc in last ch. R 2: 4 ch, 1 dc in next dc, 1 ch, 1 dc, (2 dc, 2 ch, 2 dc) in ch space, 1 dc on next dc, 1 ch, 1 dc in ch space. R 3: 3 ch, 1 dc on 3rd dc, then 2 dc, 2 ch, 2 dc (known as 1 group) in ch space, 1 dc on next dc, 1 ch, skip 1 dc, 1 dc on dc, 1 ch, 1 dc on next dc, 1 ch, 1 dc on turning ch. R 4: 4 ch, *1 dc on next dc, 1 ch, repeat from * to last 2 dc before group, skip 1 dc, 1 dc on dc, 1 group in ch space, 1 dc on next dc, 1 ch, 1 dc in ch space. R 5: 3 ch, 1 dc on 3rd dc, then group into ch space, 1 dc on next dc, skip 1 dc, *1 ch, 1 dc on dc, repeat from * and work last dc in turning ch.
Repeat R 4 and R 5 2 times more, then R 4 1 time more. R 11: 3 ch, 1 dc on 3rd dc, 1 group in ch space, 1 dc on next dc, turn.
Continue to repeat R 2–11 as required to complete one side. To turn corner, at the end of a 10th R, work only 2 dc into ch space, then 2 ch, 1 sc into the last dc of the previous R. For R 11, 2 ch for turn, 2 dc into ch space, 1 dc across the 2 dc into the sc of the 10th R. Next R: 4 ch, 1 dc in next dc, 1 ch, 1 dc, 1 group in ch space, (1 dc, 1 ch, 1 dc) in the turning ch space of the previous 9th R. Work R 3–11. Continue in pattern as before.
Press work very carefully, then sew lace edging to bedspread.

How-to

Clusters of double crochet

Clusters in between single crochet

1 Make five half-worked double crochets, keeping all of the stitches on the hook.

2 Pass the yarn around the hook and draw the loop through all six stitches on the hook.

3 Finally, make one chain and continue across the row to the next cluster in single crochet.

4 Double crochet next row. Make half-worked double crochets into 2 cluster loops; draw yarn through.

Clusters in between double crochet

1 Clusters in a different color: Make six half-worked double crochets in the cluster color, then yarn around hook in main color.

2 Draw yarn through all seven loops on the hook and continue in double crochet in main color. Work all rows from the wrong side.

In refreshing pastels

Crochet

Size: Directions are given for 88 cm or 34½" bust. Changes for 96 cm or 37½" bust are in brackets.

Materials Required:

200 (250) gm or 8 (9) oz off-white. 50 gm or 2 oz each of green and rose for either model, 50 gm or 2 oz rust for the diamond design. Crochet hook size D. 5 buttons.

Basic Pattern: R 1 (wrong side): Double crochet, turning with 3 ch. R 2: Single crochet, turning with 1 ch. These 2 R form the repeat.

Tension: 22 sts and 16 R = 10 cm or 4".

Abbreviations: Ch = chain. Sc = single crochet. Dc = double crochet. R = row(s). Rnd(s) = round(s). St(s) = stitch(es).

DIAMOND DESIGN

Back: Make 89 (97) ch and work 1 sc into 3rd ch from hook, then sc in each ch to end — 88 (96) sts. With 1st R as wrong side R, *work in sc with 3 R each of green, rose, off-white, repeat from * once, then work 3 R each of green and off-white. Change to Basic Pattern and continue in off-white, increasing 1 st each end of every 4th R 6 times — 100 (108) sts. Work straight to 26 (28) cm or 10¼" (11").

Shape Armholes: At beginning of R, decrease 4 (6) sts 2 times, 2 sts 4 times, 1 st 4 times, then decrease 1 st each end of every 2nd R 5 times — 70 (74) sts.

This waist-length vest features a diamond design in cluster stitch. See the following page for the same style in pastel stripes.

Work straight to 44 cm or 17¼".

Shape Neck: Leave center 24 sts unworked and work on each side separately. At neck edge, on every 2nd R, decrease 2 sts 2 times and 1 st 2 times. *At the same time,* at 45 cm or 17¾", on every 2nd R at armhole edge, decrease 5 (6) sts 1 time, 6 (6) sts 1 time, and 6 (7) sts 1 time.

Left Front: Make 41 (45) ch and work in sc pattern as for Back. Continue in Basic Pattern, shaping side, armhole, and shoulder to match Back. *At the same time,* follow the diagram and work clusters in position and colors as shown.

1st R (wrong side) will read: Dc 15, work cluster in next st by working 5 dc into st, but leaving last loop of each st on hook, yarn over, and draw through all loops, 1 ch, 9 dc, cluster in next st, 1 dc, cluster in next st, 9 dc, cluster in next st, 3 dc.

In next R, work 2 dc into loop and ch of each cluster, leaving last loop of each dc on hook, yarn over, and draw through loops.

Continue, following the diagram and noting that the diamond is smaller above armholes. *At the same time,* at 23 cm or 9", decrease 1 st at Front edge on every R 6 times, then on every 2nd R 8 times.

Right Front: Work to match Left Front, reversing pattern and shapings.

Finishing: Join all seams. Work 94 (98) sc around each armhole. Work 1 rnd of off-white, 3 rnds each of green and rose, 6 rnds of off-white. Fasten off.

Using off-white and beginning at lower edge of Right Front, work 50 sc up straight edges, 56 sc along curved edges to shoulders and 38 sc across Back — 250 sts. Work 3 R each of green, off-white, and rose. *At the same time,* after the 1st off-white R, work 5 buttonholes with 2 ch over 2 sc. Place the 1st one 4 sts from lower edge, and 4 more at 9 sc intervals. Sew on buttons.

STRIPED DESIGN

Work borders in off-white. Follow diagram for Stitch Pattern and Color Sequence.

▲ Vary the design with cluster stitch worked in rows and the borders worked in the main color.

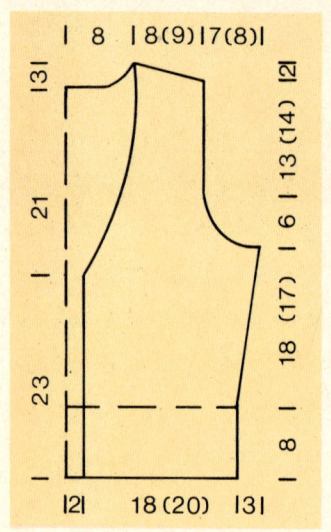

◄ Half-pattern for small (large) size. Measurements are in centimeters; inches are given in the directions.

► Crochet diagram for the diamond design. Only the odd-numbered rows are given; all even-numbered rows are worked in single crochet.

▼ Crochet diagram for the stripe design. Only the odd-numbered rows are given; all even-numbered rows are worked in single crochet. Rows 1–24 form the pattern repeat.

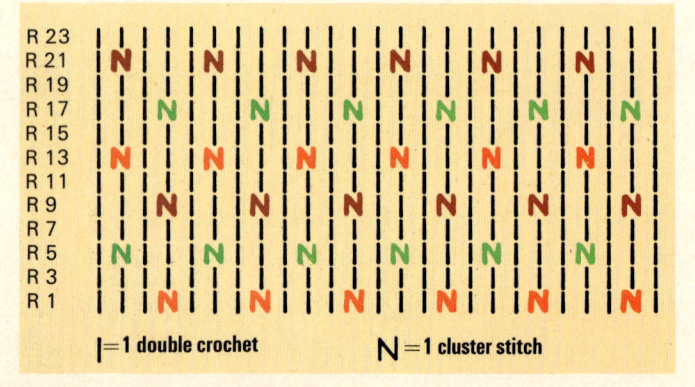

| = 1 double crochet   N = 1 cluster stitch

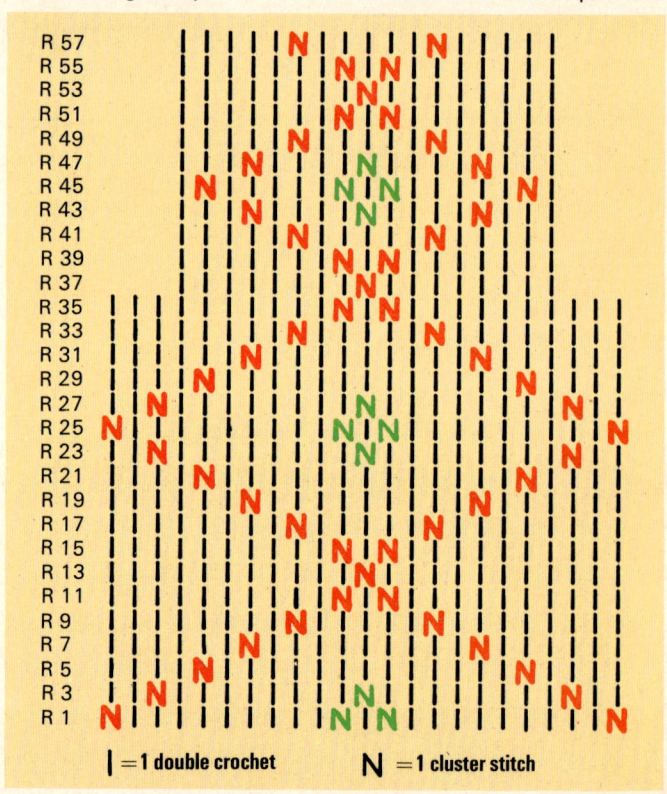

Combine beads with crochet

Crochet

Vested interest

2349

Here is something different — and much easier than it looks. The wooden beads are strung on the yarn and then crocheted onto the garment.

Size: Directions are for 84 cm or 33" bust. Changes for 92 cm or 36" bust are in brackets.

Materials Required:

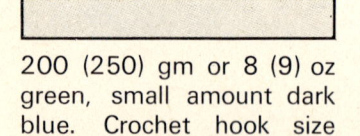

200 (250) gm or 8 (9) oz green, small amount dark blue. Crochet hook size B. Wooden beads: 72 pale blue, 128 green, and 192 dark blue.

Basic Pattern: Sc, working 1st sc into 3rd ch from hook and 1 sc into each ch to end. Turn with 1 ch.

Crochet Diagram: Each square = 1 st. Work beading in color indicated.

Tension: 30 sts and 30 R = 10 cm or 4".

Abbreviations: Ch = chain. Sc = single crochet. R = row(s). Rnd(s) = round(s).

DIRECTIONS

Back and Front: Work in one piece. Using green, make 241 (259) ch and work in sc to 19 cm or 7½".

Shape Back Armholes: Leave first and last 54 (60) sts and continue only over center 132 (138) sts for Back. At each end of every R, decrease 5 sts 1 time, 3 sts 2 times, 2 sts 2 times, 1 st 2 times, then 1 st each end of every 2nd R 4 times — 90 (96) sts. Work straight to 40 cm or 15¾".

Shape Back Neck and Shoulders: Leave center 22 sts unworked and work on each side separately. At neck edge on every R decrease 2 sts 4 times, 1 st 2 times. *At the same time,* decrease in every 2nd R at armhole edge 4 sts 3 times and 4 (5) sts 3 times.

Shape Fronts: First thread the required number of beads onto 1 ball of yarn, threading them in the correct color sequence — see diagram. Follow the How-to and Crochet Diagram, always reading the R from left to right and working a bead in on the wrong side R. Place the first bead on first wrong side R on the 18th (24th) st from either front edge. *At the same time,* shape armhole and shoulder to match Back. At 23 cm or 9", decrease 1 st at front edge on next R and every 6th (5th) R 8 (11) times.

Finishing: Join shoulders. Using dark blue, work 140 sc around each armhole. Work 1 rnd of sc on sc. Fasten off. Work the same edging around Fronts; work 68 sc up straight edges, 60 sts up shaped edges, and 44 sc across Back neck.

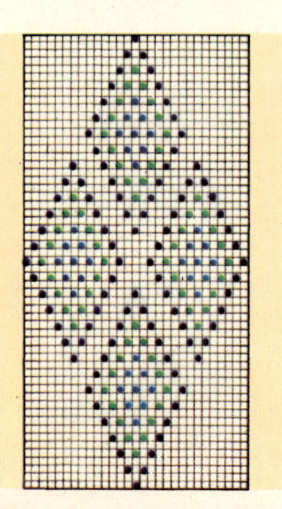

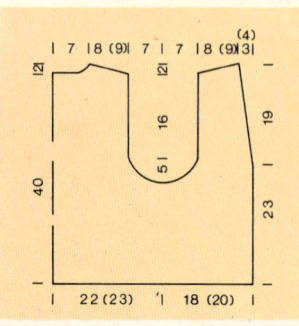

Half-pattern for front/back piece in small (large) size. The numbers are centimeters; inches are in directions.

◄ **Crochet Diagram:** Each square = 1 stitch. Each color = 1 colored bead.

How-to

Crocheting with beads

1 First, dip the end of the yarn in wax to avoid fraying. When threading the beads, follow the Crochet Diagram from top to bottom and from left to right. Rewind the yarn fairly loosely to allow for the free rows between beads.

2 Always crochet beads on a wrong side row. Insert the hook into the stitch, draw loop through from behind the bead and slip both loops off together.

3 Position the first bead where indicated in the directions. For all other rows, follow the crochet diagram for the correct placement of the beads.

Strawberry time

Play your part in the revival of the peasant look with this crocheted bolero decorated in a charming strawberry pattern.

How-to

Strawberry pattern

The strawberries are made by working a knob pattern in two colors.

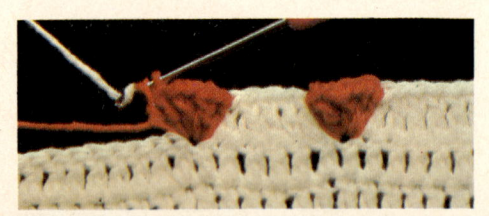

1 R 1: (right side) Work strawberry in red. Work 5 dc, (1 dc, 1 ch) 4 times and 1 dc in 6th st. When changing color, the last st of one color is always looped off with the new color.

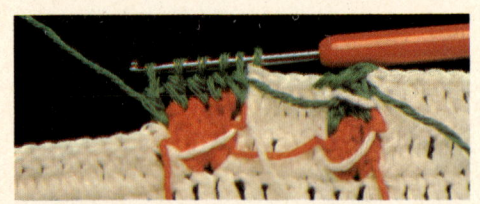

2 R 2: Work dc in dc of main color and in every red dc, work 1 half-finished green dc ...

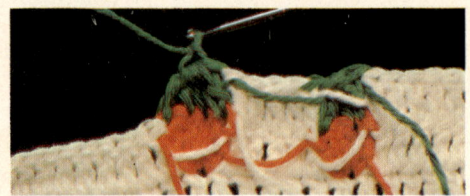

3 ... then loop off all 6 loops together and work 1 ch in green to secure the loops.

4 In the next R, work the strawberries in transposed order, always working 5 dc in main color between the strawberries.

Size: Directions are for 84 cm or 33" bust. Changes for 92 cm or 36" bust are in brackets.

Materials Required:

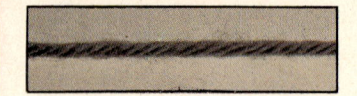

200 (250) gm or 8 (9) oz black, 50 gm or 2 oz each green and red [50 gm = 110 m or 120 yds]. Crochet hook size E.

Basic Stitch: Dc. Every R begins after 3 turning ch in 2nd st and ends on 3rd turning ch of previous R.

Strawberry Pattern: R 1: (right side) 3 ch in black to turn, *then in next st in red work (1 dc, 1 ch) 4 times, and 1 dc, then 1 dc in black in each of next 5 sts, repeat from *, but end 1 dc in black instead of 5 dc. R 2: 3 ch in black for turn, *then in green work 1 half-finished dc in each red dc and loop off all 6 loops together, 1 ch to fasten, then 5 dc in black, repeat from *, ending last repeat 1 dc in black instead of 5 dc. Repeat R 1 and 2, but transpose strawberries (ie, next R: 3 ch, 3 black dc, then Strawberry Pattern).

Tension: 20 sts and 10 R = 10 cm or 4".

Abbreviations: Ch = chain. Sc = single crochet. Dc = double crochet. St(s) = stitch(es). R = row(s).

DIRECTIONS

Left Front: Using black, make 33 (37) ch and work straight in Basic Stitch to 22 (23) cm or 8½" (9"). Now at beginning of right edge, after the 3 turning ch, work 1st strawberry, then in every 2nd R work 1 more strawberry into the Basic Stitch, alternating them (note fabric is widened with insertion of motifs). *At the same time,* at 31 (33) cm or 12" (13"), shape neck on every R by decreasing 2 sts 1 time and 1 st 2 (4) times — 26 (28) sts. When there are 18 R of Strawberry Pattern in all, leave piece aside. Front measures about 39 (41) cm or 15" (16").

Right Front: As Left Front, reversing strawberry placement and shapings.

Back: Return to Left Front and work 2 R, increasing 1 st at neck edge on each R. *At the same time,* work Strawberry Pattern to match Front by reversing red and green. Now work 2 R on Right Front, make 20 (24) ch in black for back neck, and work across all sts, decreasing strawberries until 1 strawberry remains each end. Now continue in dc in black to 78 (82) cm or 30" (32"). Fasten off.

Finishing: Pin out and steam-press. With wrong side facing, work 62 (66) sc along each front edge. In next 2 R, work the Strawberry Pattern, working dc in sc of previous R and decreasing 1 st at neck edge on each R — 60 (64) sts. Work 2 R sc in green, 2 R Strawberry Pattern, alternating strawberries and reversing colors, 1 R sc in black. With wrong side facing and black, work 68 (72) sc on each armhole edge, 1 R sc on sc, fasten off. With green, work 12 R sc around neck. Sew up side seams. Work 2 R in green along lower edges.

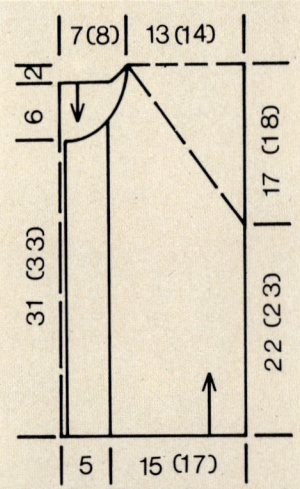

Half-pattern for small (large) size. Numbers are centimeters; inches are in directions. Work in direction of arrows.

Crochet

Step out in style

Is this a cardigan, a jacket, or a coat? Or is it all three? However you choose to interpret this design, it will keep you warm from one end of the year to the other and you will always look smart. Note the front buttoning, the optional tie belt, and the stylish turn-back collar.

Size: Directions are for 92 cm or 36" bust. Changes for 100 cm or 39½" bust are in brackets.

Materials Required:

1500 (1600) gm or 53 (57) oz blue [100 gm = 96 m or 105 yds]. Crochet hook size K. 5 buttons.

Basic Pattern: R 1: *Draw out 2 loops from the 4th st from hook (i.e. draw 1 loop from back, then hook through front of st and draw through another loop), skip 1 st, then insert hook into back and front of the next st as before, yarn over hook, and draw through the 5 loops on hook (called the slip-off loop), 2 ch (1 group completed), repeat from *, but work beginning of each repeat into the last insertion place of last group and end with ½ group by working 2 loops into last st of previous group, yarn over, and draw through the 3 loops on hook, 1 ch, 1 dc in last st, turn with 3 ch. R 2: *Draw 2 loops as before from the 1st slip-off loop of previous R, then 2 loops from next slip-off loop of next group, yarn over, and draw through all 5 loops. Continue in this way, ending R by drawing 2 loops from previous group, yarn over, and draw through 3 loops, 1 ch, 1 dc in turning ch. Repeat R 2.

Tension: 4½ groups and 6 R = 10 cm or 4".

Abbreviations: Ch = chain. Dc = double crochet. Sc = single crochet. St(s) = stitch(es). R = row(s).

DIRECTIONS

Back: Make 55 (59) ch and work in Basic Pattern — 26 (28) groups. Work 6 R.

▲ You can wear your cardigan buttoned and tied as shown here, to really keep the winter chill at bay.

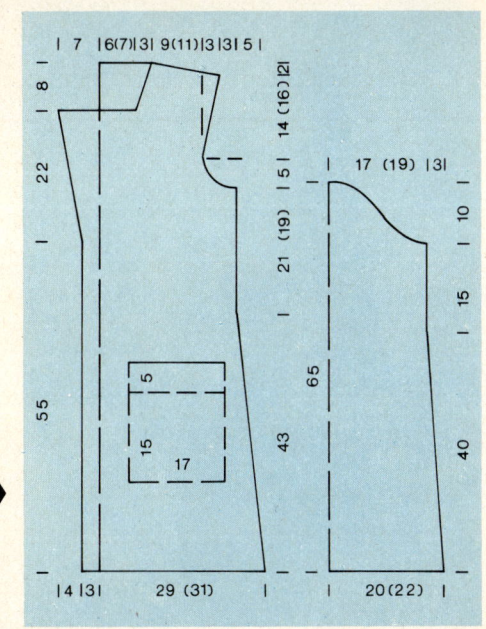

▶ Half-pattern for small (large) size. The numbers are centimeters; inches are given in the directions.

2353

And here you can see the cardigan open and worn more casually. The design is so practical that you'll find yourself wearing it with almost everything – and loving it!

In next R, decrease ½ group each end thus: 1 dc into 1st slip-off loop, then ½ group into next slip-off loop and continue in pattern, omitting last ½ group and working 1 ch, 1 dc, 3 ch, turn. Work in pattern, decreasing ½ group each end of every 6th R 3 times more – 22 (24) groups. Work straight to 64 (62) cm or 25" (24½").

Shape Armholes: Decrease 1½ groups each end of next R, then ½ group each end of next 2 R – 17 (19) groups. Now increase ½ group each end of the 2nd R and following 4th R by working 1 group from the dc and next slip-off loop – 19 (21) groups. Continue straight to 83 cm or 32½".

Shape Shoulders: Decrease 3 (3) groups at beginning of next R by slip-stitching along work at beginning of R and leaving last 3 (3) groups unworked at end of R, then decrease 2½ (3) groups at each end of next R – 8 (9) groups remain. Fasten off.

Pocket Linings: For each, make 20 ch and work 1st sc into 3rd ch from hook; work in sc for 15 cm or 6". Leave for the present.

Left Front: Make 31 (33) ch and work in Basic Pattern – 14 (15) groups. Shape side, armhole and shoulder as for Back. *At the same time,* work straight at front edge to 30 cm or 11¾", ending at side edge. Work across 2 groups, then work across the 18 sc of Pocket Lining in pattern, skip 9 groups of Left Front, work pattern to end. Continue to work shapings as for Back, keeping front edge straight to 55 cm or

$21\frac{3}{4}$", ending at front edge. Shape lapel by increasing $\frac{1}{2}$ group at beginning of next R and every 4th R 3 times. At 77 cm or $30\frac{1}{4}$", leave $5\frac{1}{2}$ (6) groups at front edge unworked, then at neck edge decrease $\frac{1}{2}$ group on every 2nd R 3 times. Go back to Pocket top and work across the 9 unworked groups in sc for 5 cm or 2". Fasten off.

Right Front: Work to match Left Front, reversing shapings.

Sleeves: Make 39 (43) ch and work in Basic Pattern – 18 (20) groups. Continue in pattern, decreasing $\frac{1}{2}$ group each end in every 8th R 3 times – 15 (17) groups. Work straight to 55 cm or $21\frac{1}{2}$".

Shape Top: At each end of every R decrease 2 groups 1 time, 1 group 1 time, $\frac{1}{2}$ group 2 times, 1 group 1 time and 2 groups 1 time – 1 (3) groups remain. Fasten off.

Belt: Make 10 ch and work 1 dc into 4th ch from hook, then 1 dc into each ch. Turn each R with 3 ch and work dc on dc for 160 cm or 63". Fasten off.

Finishing: Join seams, sewing the lower sleeve seam from right side for 10 cm or 4" for turn-back. Sew pocket linings in place. For collar, begin and end 7 cm or $2\frac{3}{4}$" from lapel edges and work in Basic Pattern for 10 cm or 4", working 1st R into fabric evenly. Fasten off.
Work 1 R of sc along each front edge, lapel edges, and short ends of collar. Fasten off.
Sew 5 buttons in position as shown in photograph, using the holes in pattern as buttonholes.

How-to

Star stitch

1 Holding the yarn at the front of the work, insert hook into the slip-off loop of the previous R from back to front and draw up a long loop from front of work.

2 Holding the yarn at the back of the work, insert hook again into the same slip-off loops from front to back and draw another long loop through.

3 Insert hook into the following slip-off loop from back to front, drawing a loop through as before.

4 Insert hook again into the same slip-off loop, this time from front to back and draw a loop through.

5 Now pass the yarn over the hook and draw it through all 5 loops on the hook, work 2 ch. Directions and photographs 1–5 form 1 group. Repeat required number of times.

6 For next group, draw the first 2 loops from the last point of insertion of the previous group, and the next 2 loops from the following slip-off loop.

Country stroller

Stride out and beat the cold in our chunky jacket and matching pull-on hat. The tie-around belt ensures a trim shape for the jacket so that you can team it with various outfits.

Size: Directions are for 92 cm or 36" bust. Changes for 100 cm or $39\frac{1}{2}$" are in brackets.

Materials Required:

Jacket: 1200 (1300) gm or 43 (46) oz red. Hat: 200 gm or 8 oz red. [50 gm = 75 m or 82 yds]. Crochet hook size I. 5 buttons.

Basic Pattern 1: R 1: (right side) Beginning in the 2nd st from hook, sc across. R 2 and all wrong side R: 1 ch for turn, then 1 sc into 1st st and all sts to end. R 3: 1 ch for turn, 1 sc into 1st st, *1 relief dc into each of 2 sc of the previous *right* side R (worked thus: yarn around hook, then with hook at front of work take hook around sc from right to left and draw loop through, then continue as a normal dc), 1 sc on each of next 2 sts of previous R, repeat from *, ending 2 relief dc, 1 sc in last st. R 5: Repeat R 3, but work the relief dc around the relief dc of previous R. R 7: 1 ch for turn, 1 sc into 1st st, *2 sc, 2 relief dc around sc of previous R, repeat from *, ending 3 sc. R 9: Repeat R 7, but work relief dc around relief dc of previous R. Repeat R 3–10.

Basic Pattern 2: Sc.

Tension 1: 13 sts and 13 R = 10 cm or 4".

Tension 2: 13 sts and 15 R = 10 cm or 4".

Abbreviations: Ch = chain. Sc = single crochet. Dc = double crochet. R = row(s). Rnd(s) = round(s). St(s) = stitch(es).

JACKET

Back: Make 73 (79) ch and work in Basic Pattern 1, beginning and ending R 3 with 1 (2) sc and working 2 relief dc each end of R 7 for 2nd size. Work in pattern to 5 cm or 2", then decrease 1 st at each end of next R and every 9th R 4 times – 62 (68) sts. Work straight to 54 (53) cm or $21\frac{1}{4}$" ($20\frac{3}{4}$").

Shape Armholes: At each end of every R decrease 3 (4) sts 1 time, 2 sts 1 time, 1 st 1 time, then 1 st each end of every 2nd R 2 times – 46 (50) sts. Work straight to 65 cm or $25\frac{1}{2}$", then change to Basic Pattern 2 and continue to 72 cm or $28\frac{1}{4}$".

Shape Neck: Leave center 10 sts unworked and continue on each side separately. At neck edge, on every R decrease 2 sts 1 time and 1 st 3 times. *At the same time*, at 73 cm or $28\frac{3}{4}$", in every R at armhole edge decrease 4 (5) sts 2 times and 5 sts 1 time.

Left Front: Make 35 (38) ch and work in Basic Pattern 1, beginning 3rd R as 7th R of Back and ending R with 1 (3) sc. Continue in pattern as set, and work stitches and shapings as for Back, but shape front edge at 50 cm or $19\frac{1}{2}$". Decrease 1 st on next front edge R, then 1 st on every 6th R 3 times and 1 st on every 4th R 4 times.

Right Front: Work as for Left Front, reversing ends of R and shapings.

Sleeves: Make 41 (44) ch and work in Basic Pattern 2 on the 40 (43) sc to 12 cm or $4\frac{3}{4}$". Change to Basic Pattern 1 and work as for Left Front, increasing 1 st each end of every 14th R 3 times – 46 (49) sts. Work straight to 46 cm or $18\frac{1}{2}$".

Shape Top: At each end of R, decrease 3 (4) sts 1 time, 2 sts 2 times, 1 st 1 time, 1 st each end of every 2nd R 4 times. Then at each end of R, decrease 1 st 1 time, 2 sts 2 times, and 3 sts 1 time. Work across the 6 (7) sts; fasten off.

Pockets: (make 2) Make 21 ch and work in Basic Pattern 1 to 16 cm or $16\frac{1}{4}$", then work 4 cm or $1\frac{1}{2}$" in Basic Pattern 2. Fasten off.

Collar/Band: Make 27 ch and work in Basic Pattern 2 and shape sides each end of every R by increasing 1 st 3 times, then 2 sts 15 times. Make 65 ch each end for front bands – 222 sts. Work straight for 2 cm or $\frac{3}{4}$", ending at Right Front edge. Next R: Work 8 sts from edge then for 1st buttonhole work 3 ch, skip 3 sts. Work 4 more buttonholes at 10 cm or 4" intervals. Work straight until Band measures 4 cm or $1\frac{1}{2}$". Fasten off.

Belt: Make 6 ch and work 140 cm or 55" in Basic Pattern 2. Fasten off.

Finishing: Press on wrong side. Join seams, joining lower 8 cm or 3" of Sleeve from right side for turnback of cuff. Sew Collar/Band to front and neck edge. Sew on Pockets 5 cm or 2" from lower edge. Sew on buttons.

HAT

Make 68 ch and join into a ring with a slip st. Continue working in rnds, beginning each rnd with 1 ch, and join each rnd with a slip st. Work in Basic Pattern 2 to 20 cm or 10", then change and work in Basic Pattern 1 from * to * of each R. At 33 cm or 13", decrease for crown. On next pattern rnd, work together the 2 sc between relief dc – 51 sts. In next pattern rnd, work the 2 relief dc as half-finished relief dc; loop them off together all around – 34 sts. In next pattern rnd, work 1 half-finished relief dc, then 1 sc, looping them off together – 17 sts. Work 1 rnd of dc, then in next rnd work in half-finished dc, looping them off together. Draw up remaining sts and fasten off securely.

Half-pattern for small (large) size. Crochet Collar/Band in the direction of the arrow. Numbers are in centimeters; inches are in the directions.

Here you see a back view (inset) of the jacket and hat. Note how the jacket comes well down over the hips. The waist is nipped in with a tie belt.

Diamonds in double crochet

How-to

Relief double crochet is used to create a three-dimensional crochet pattern.

R 1: (wrong side) Make 2 dc into the 5th ch from the hook, *skip 1 ch, 2 dc into the next ch, repeat from *.

R 2: (right side) 3 ch for turn, 1 group (2 dc in the spaces between the pairs of dc of the previous R) into the next 2 spaces, *2 relief dc around the 1st dc of the 2nd following pair of dc on the right side of the piece, 2 relief dc around the 2nd dc of the same pair, skip one pair of dc, work 1 group into each of the following 5 spaces, repeat from *, ending with 1 group into each of the last 4 spaces.

R 3: (wrong side) 3 ch for turn, work 1 group into each of the next 3 spaces, *1 relief dc around the 1st pair of relief dc, 1 group between the 2 pairs of relief dc, 2 relief dc around the 2nd pair of relief dc, work 1 group into each of the following 4 spaces, repeat from *, ending with 1 group into each of the last 3 spaces.

R 4–7: Repeat R 3, moving the relief dc 1 group to the right or left in each R to form diamonds. There will now be 4 adjacent relief dc.

R 8: The relief dc are crossed thus: 3 ch for turn, 1 group into the next space, 1 relief dc around each of the relief dc at the edge, *1 group into each of the next 5 spaces, 1 relief dc each around the next 3rd and 4th relief dc, then 1 relief dc each around the 1st and 2nd relief dc, repeat from *, ending with 1 relief dc around each of the relief dc at the edge, and 1 group into the last space.

R 9: 3 ch for turn, 1 group in the next space, 2 relief dc, 1 group into each of next 4 spaces, repeat from * of R 3, ending 2 relief dc and 1 group into the last space.

R 10–13: Repeat R 4–7. There are now 4 relief dc adjacent to each other.

R 14: 3 ch for turn, work 1 group into each of the next 4 spaces, *cross the relief dc as for R 8, work 1 group into each of the next 5 spaces, repeat from *, ending with crossed relief dc and 1 group into each of the next 3 spaces. Repeat R 3–14, remembering to begin each new repeat of the pattern with 3 groups as in R 3 to bring the pattern back into position and avoid distortion.

Size: Directions are for 108 cm or 42½". chest. Changes for 117 cm or 46" chest are in brackets.

Materials Required:

950 (1050) gm or 34 (38) oz beige. Crochet hook size E. 7 buttons.

Basic Stitch: See How-to.
Tension: 16 sts and 10 R = 10 cm or 4".
Abbreviations: Ch = chain. Sc = single crochet. Dc = double crochet. St(s) = stitch(es). R = row(s).

DIRECTIONS

Back: Make 92 (100) ch and work 4 cm or 1½" in sc – 91 (99) sts. Continue in Basic Stitch, but for 2nd size, work 2 extra groups each end in every R. Work straight to 46 cm or 18".

Shape Armholes: Keeping continuity of pattern, at each end of every R, decrease 4 (6) sts 1 time and 2 sts 3 times – 69 (73) sts. Work straight to 67 (68) cm or 26¼" (26¾").

Shape Neck: Leave center 25 sts unworked and work on each side separately. At neck edge, in every R decrease 2 sts 2 times. *At the same time,* at 68 (69) cm or 26¾" (27") at armhole edge, in every 2nd R decrease 9 (10) sts 2 times.

Left Front: Make 50 (54) ch and work 4 cm or 1½" in sc – 49 (53) sts. Continue in Basic Stitch, but for 2nd size work 2 extra groups at side edge only. Shape armhole as for Back and continue straight to 58 (59) cm or 22¾" (23¼"), ending at front edge.

Shape Neck: At front edge, in every R decrease 7 sts 1 time, 2 sts 4 times, and 1 st 3 times. Continue straight to 68 (69) cm or 26¾" (27"), then shape shoulder as for Back.

Right Front: Match Left Front, reversing shapings.

Sleeves: Make 50 (50) ch and work 4 cm or 1½" in sc – 49 sts. Change to Basic Stitch and increase 1 st each end of

For crochet experts
A man's best friend

every 5th (4th). R 8 (10) times — 65 (69) sts. (Always work dc on dc for 1st increase, then in pattern when 2 dc (1 group) has been increased). Work straight to 47 cm or 18½".

Shape Top: At each end of every R, decrease 4 sts 1 time, 2 sts 3 times, 1 st 7 (8) times, 2 sts 3 times, 4 sts 1 time — 11 (13) sts. Fasten off.

Finishing: Press pieces. Join all seams. Work 94 (96) sc up straight part of each Front edge and 88 sts around neck edge. Work in sc, working 3 sc into each corner st at neck on each R and decreasing 4 sts evenly around neck edge on every 2nd R. *At the same time,* at 2 cm or ¾", work buttonholes over 4 sts, placing the first one 1.5 cm or ⅝" from Left Front edge, the 2nd one 6 (7) cm or 2¼" (2¾") away, and 5 more at 7 cm or 2¾" intervals. Work to 4 cm or 1½" and fasten off. Sew on buttons.

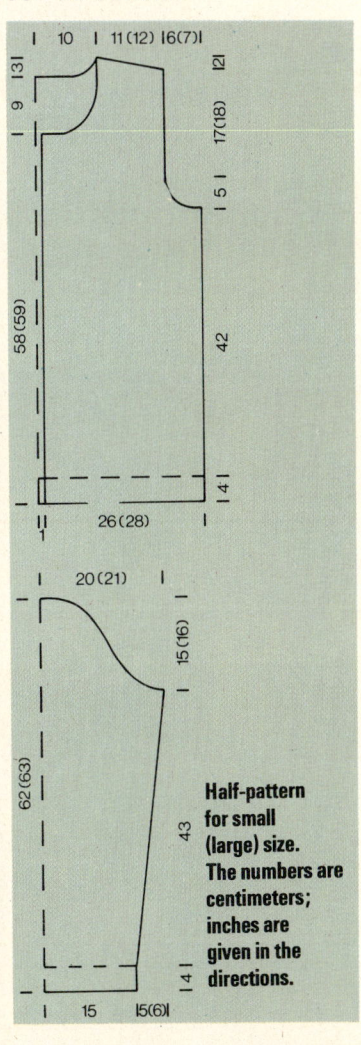

Half-pattern for small (large) size. The numbers are centimeters; inches are given in the directions.

Style 1

Style 2

Style 3

Illustrated Sewing 73

Dress through the ages

Here we feature five summer dresses which are versatile enough for home or school. The patterns are on Pattern Sheet 73. For sizes (age range is 3 to 12 years) see Body Measurements Chart on the pattern sheet.

Style 1: (in sizes W and Y) The effect of this smart and sophisticated dress is created by the combination of fabrics — plain and patterned. All the seams have been trimmed with scarlet, while the patch pockets on the skirt have piped openings. Use toggles for the front fastening.

Style 2: (in sizes S and U) Here's a princess style in a summery gingham. The seams and patch pockets are piped, there is a zipper down the front, and an inverted pleat.

Style 3: (in sizes T and V) All small girls like to feel pretty and feminine, so here is just the dress to put her in the mood. Made up here in a flowery print, the bodice is tucked and top-stitched in a contrasting color. There are decorative buttons, plus white collar and cuffs trimmed with braid.

Style 4: (in sizes CQ and S) Shirt dresses are always useful, worn on their own or over pants. Make this one in stripes, then trim it with the collar and cuffs in a plain color. Round off the side slits — tomboy style.

Style 5: (in sizes CP and R) Finally, here's a pretty dress covered in flowers and trimmed with rickrack. Note the wing sleeves, belt, and pockets. She'll just love it!

Style 5

Style 4

Inserting a corded piping

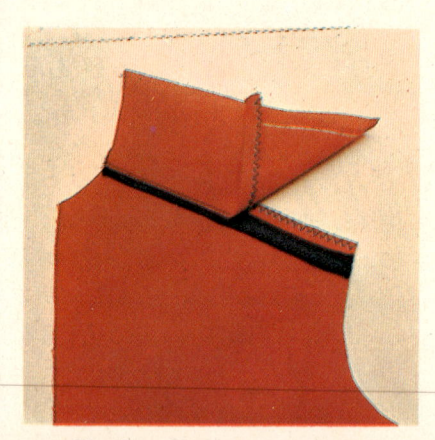

1 If trimming inner seams, such as those on yokes and cuffs, work as shown here. Begin by finishing the raw edges, then pin the corded piping to one piece with the flat side toward the seam allowance and the raised part beyond the seamline. Stitch the piping in place, without stitching into the cording itself. Press the seam allowances of the second piece to the inside, place over the piping, pin in place, and then stitch close to the edge, using the zipper presser foot.

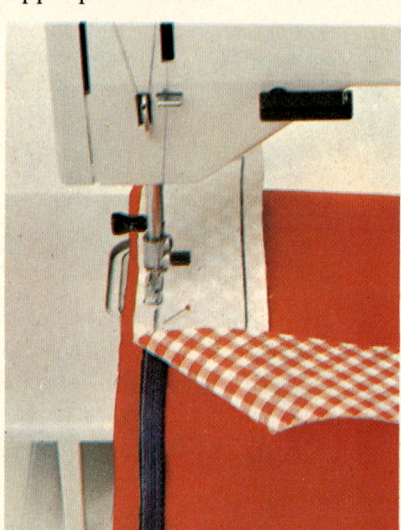

2 Here, a band is being stitched to the front border so that the piping is caught between. Stitch the piping in place as shown in photograph 1, then pin and stitch the band along the marked seamline, right sides facing, close to the raised part of the cording. Use the zipper presser foot when stitching. The zipper presser foot varies from machine to machine. If there is a groove in one side of the foot only, this means that the needle cannot be moved. In this case, place the fabric so that the greater part of the fabric lies to the right of the needle. If there are two grooves, however, you can adjust the foot so that the needle is in the left groove. This means that the greater part of the fabric will lie to the left of the needle and there is less fabric running through the machine.
If top-stitching is required, work it at this stage.

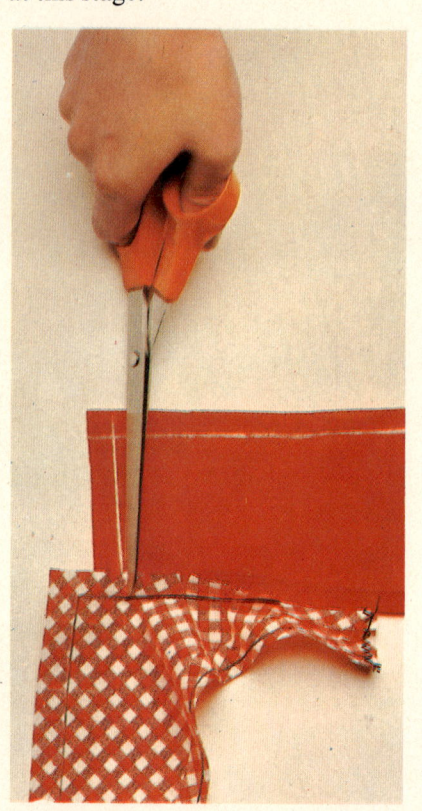

3 Press the seam allowance of the inside edge of the facing to the inside, then stitch close to the edge. Finish the shoulder seam allowance. Stitch the upper collar to the facing where marked, right sides together. Do not stitch beyond the seam allowance. Clip into the seam allowance of the facing only at each end, clipping down to the last stitch as shown above. Press open the neck seam at the front, but at the back, press the seam allowance upward. Stitch the under collar to the bodice, right sides facing, then clip into the seam allowance of the bodice only.

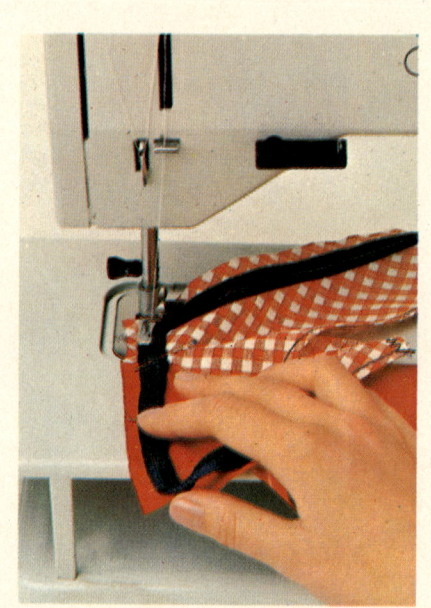

4 Pin piping to the facing and the upper collar, making sure that the flat side is toward the seam allowance. Work on a firm base so that the piping is not pulled out of shape. Stitch from the edge of the hem to the corner of the band at the neck. Leaving the needle in the fabric, turn the work so that the top of the band and the narrow end of the collar are in a line (this is made possible by the clipping in photograph 3). Continue to stitch all around.

How-to

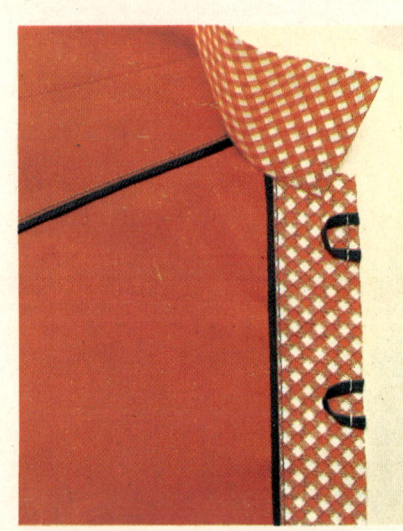

5 To make the button loops, cut bias strips 2 cm (¾") wide; the length will depend on the size of the buttons. Make all the loops as one long strip, then cut them apart. Fold the strip in half lengthwise, then fold the raw edges into the center fold and press. Stitch along long open edge. Cut the loops and pin them to the underlap band where indicated. Stitch along the seamline.

6 Stitch the band and the under collar together with the upper collar and the piping all around. The corners of the collar are worked as shown in photograph 4. Take care not to stitch into the cording inside the piping at the corners. Trim the seam allowances diagonally at the corners so that the corners will lie flat when turned. Turn to the right side.

7 If you want to top-stitch the dress, stitch around the bands and the collar close to the edge. Sew down the upper collar by hand, working into the seamline along the center back. Sew down the facing from the hem to the waist. Finally, sew on the buttons.

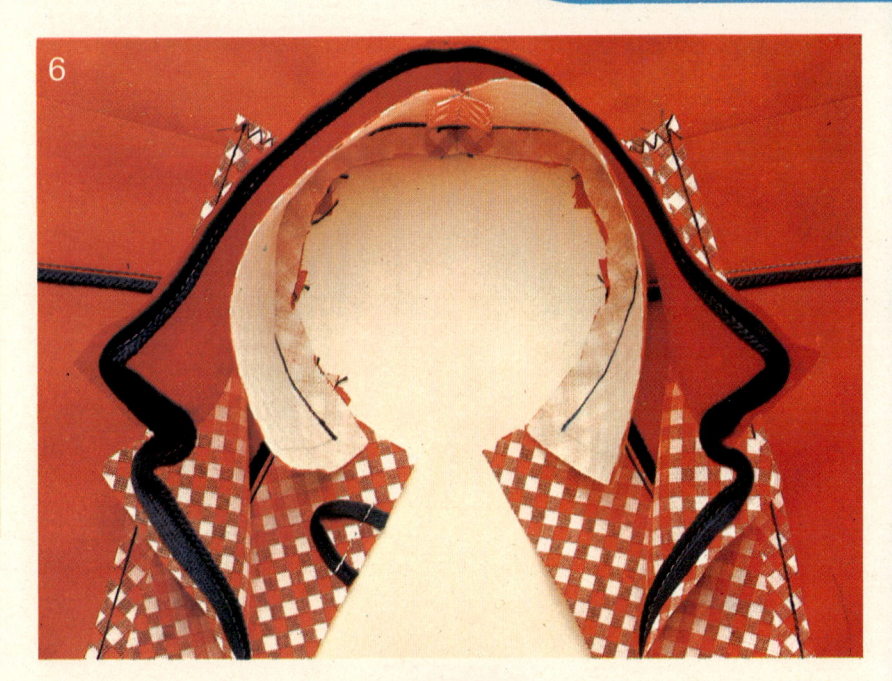

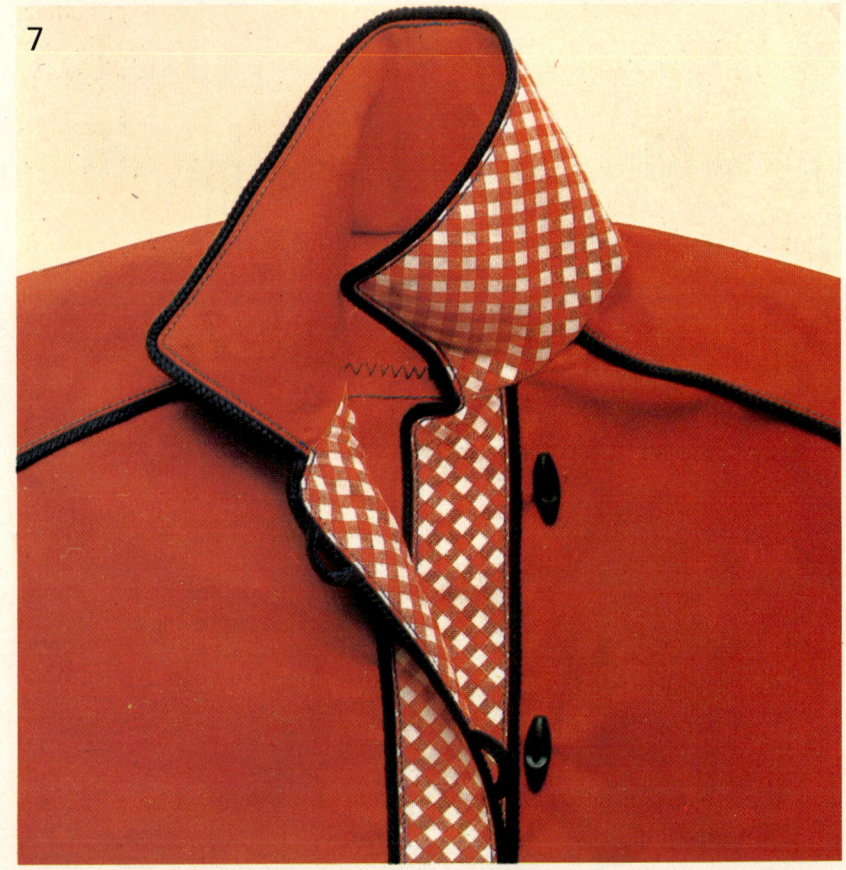

Defy the elements

Style 1

Style 2

Illustrated Sewing 74

For those days when the weather turns really nasty, we present a canvas jacket, a coat in plastic-coated fabric, and a shower-proof windbreaker. All styles are on Pattern Sheet 74.

Style 1 is an easy-to-wear jacket in sizes C and E. Simply cut, it has plenty of width so that you can wear lots of layers underneath, and it is long enough to give plenty of protection from wind and the occasional shower. There are deep yokes on the front and back and the front button band extends up into a simple turn-back collar. The sleeves are set onto the drop shoulders and sport wide cuffs. A tie-belt completes the look.

Style 2 is a fabulous raincoat in sizes C and E. It is, in fact, a longer version of Style 1 to make in plastic-coated fabric. The large, practical hood has draw strings, as have the sleeves. The coat is light and could be carried rolled up in a bag, ready for use. The detail below shows the deep yoke at the back of the coat and the amount of ease and room in the armholes.

Style 3 is for sporting enthusiasts in sizes B and D. The design is straight, roomy, and comfortable and should be made up in a light weather-proof fabric, such as the one used for making sails. You can buy this type of fabric in sailing and yachting shops. Details about working with this kind of fabric are given on the right. This style slips on over the head and elastic at the wrists and hem keeps you warm and dry. The front inset is cut in one with the hood as shown below.

Style 3

How-to

Working with woven plastic fabric

Sails these days are no longer made of coarse cotton canvas, but lightweight synthetics that throw off water and resist wind and rain. We made Style 3 in such a fabric, in this case a nylon/polyester weave. Here are a few tips to help you cope with any problems that may arise. To begin, cut this type of fabric through a single layer at a time. If you try cutting it double, you will find the fabric slides about. Try not to use pins more than absolutely necessary. Instead, fasten the parts together with clear tape. This will also keep the pattern lying flat. Finally, mark the outlines with chalk, then, if you make a mistake, you can simply wipe away your error with a damp cloth.

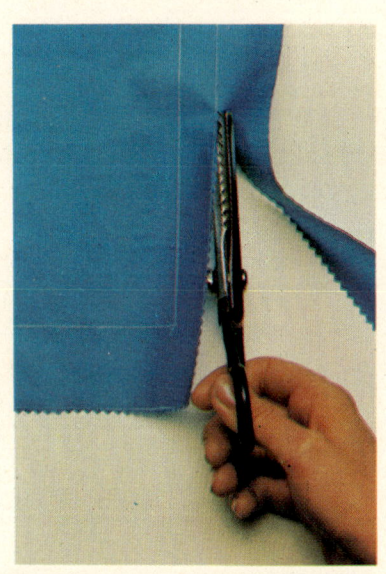

1 As the edges cannot be finished in the usual way, cut them with pinking shears. Note that the fabric will not fray if it is cut on the straight of the grain.

2 When placing two parts together, such as on the side seams, begin by pinning the corners (*outside* the seamline to avoid marks showing!). Place the remaining pins diagonally into the seam allowances. Stitch with long, loose stitches. Tight stitching could tear the fabric during wear. Test the stitch length and tension on a scrap of fabric first.

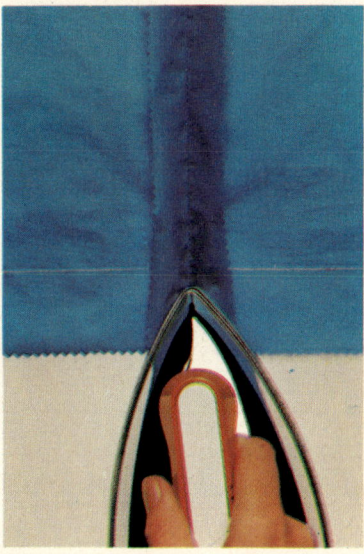

3 You can press this type of fabric with a cool iron. If the color changes, you will have to press the whole garment, as the discoloration will not disappear.

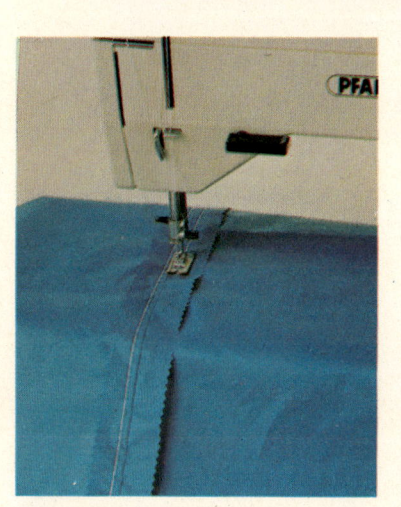

4 When you press, small "waves" may form. You can, of course, avoid pressing altogether, by stitching down the seam allowances as shown above. Test on a scrap first to decide the best approach.

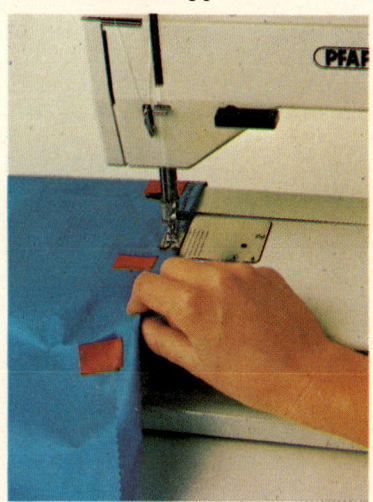

5 On edges which have to be turned to the inside, such as on the hood and hem, turn in the seam allowances and stick them down with small pieces of clear tape. Stitch the seam in the usual way with a long, loose stitch. Note that we have used colored tape here for clarity. The tape can then be pulled away.

City sophisticate

Style 1

Style 2

Style 1: Our first shirt is made up in a finely striped cotton. Long and straight, it has side slits and a three-button fastening in the front. The top photograph shows the patch pockets and the bottom one the shoulder yoke and gathered back. Also note the low shoulder line and the fact that the shirt looks just as good unbelted as belted.
Style 2: To go with the shirt, there's a straight skirt in a striped flannel with a side slit detail.

These styles are the last word in classic good taste. Choose from a long-line shirt with a matching skirt, a dress, and a sleeveless jacket and skirt. You can make them all in sizes C and E from Pattern Sheet 75.

Illustrated Sewing 75

Style 3

Style 3: Here's a dress which, when made up in a flowered fabric, will keep you looking pretty through the day and well into the evening. Cut in one piece, it has a pleat in the front, a button fastening, and a small stand-up collar. The sleeves are gathered onto narrow cuffs and the bottom photograph above shows the back gathered onto the deep yoke. Wear the dress with a matching shirt or without — it looks good either way!

2369

Style 4: This plain shirt is made from the same pattern as the striped one on the previous page. The only difference is that it is buttoned all the way down the front instead of only half way.
Style 5: The checked skirt is straight with deep side slits.
Style 6: Add a sleeveless jacket in a striped fabric in colors that echo the checked shirt. The jacket has no front fastenings. The edges and armholes are bound with bias strips, while the yoke is cut on the cross.

Bias-cut bindings

Bias-cut strips are often used to bind edges to decorative effect, and they are pressed into shape with a specially drawn template.

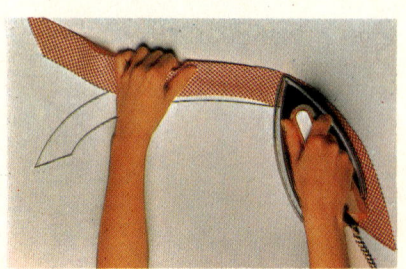

1 Trace the template onto thin cardboard or thick paper. Cut the bias strips double the width of the template, plus seam allowances. For the correct length, measure along the center of the template, standing the tape measure on edge, and add seam allowances. Fold strips in half lengthwise. With fold on outside edge, press into shape.

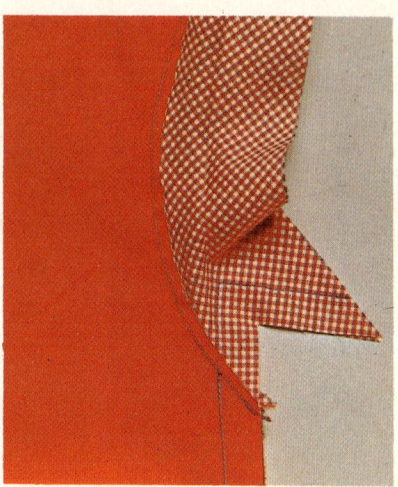

2 Stitch one layer of fabric to the armhole edge, right sides facing, checking that the seam allowance is the same width all around. Press the seam allowances toward the strip. Stitch the side seam up to the fold of the bias strip, then stitch toward outside edge at a right angle as shown. Finish the edges if the garment is not being lined.

How-to

3 Press open the seam and pin the bands together. Turn in seam allowance on other edge and fold strip to wrong side. If necessary, trim seam allowances to 1cm ($\frac{3}{8}''$). Stitch from right side through seam.

2 Stitch the center front seam to the end of the opening. Cut into the underlap as far as the fold line as shown in the photograph above. Finish edges of the cut.

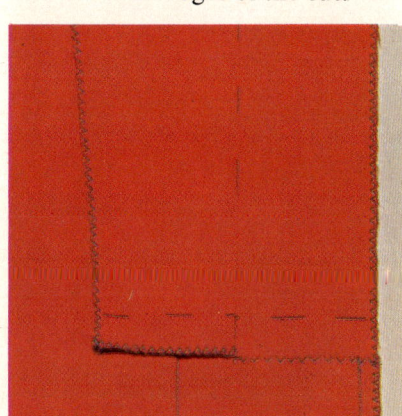

pins, turn the work and stitch up the marked line of the center seam. Leave the pins as before and turn the work again and stitch the underlap onto the overlap facing. Press the overlap facing to the left side along the marked line.

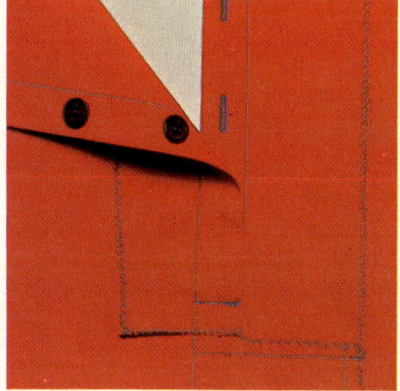

Button fastening on a pleat

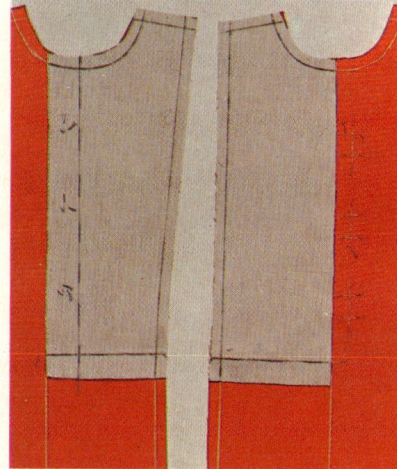

3 Stitch the pleat seam to about 10cm (4") above the hem. Press the pleat fold and press the underlap facing to the inside along the fold line. Finish the edges of the facings, finishing the overlap facing together with the pleat.

5 Stitch through all the layers working into overlap and underlap from the inside along the existing seam. Top-stitch the underlap along the extension of the center back seam; top-stitch the overlap to the same width. If using a non-iron interfacing, top-stitch again near the fold edge to give a firm finish. Work buttonholes and sew on buttons.

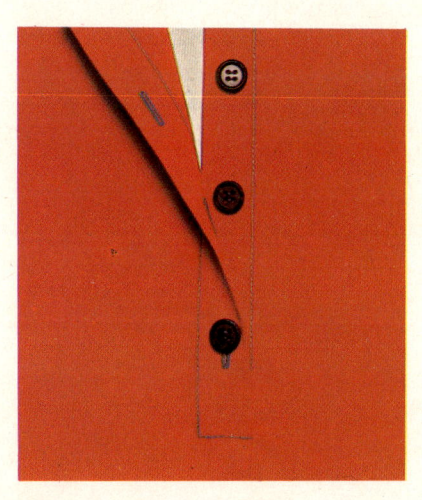

1 To begin, interface the facing with a piece the length of the opening, plus 2cm ($\frac{3}{4}''$) on the lower edge, no seam allowance on the front edge, and 1cm ($\frac{3}{8}''$) elsewhere. Choose an interfacing suitable for the fabric being used. Iron an iron-on interfacing into place or baste on non-iron interfacing. Mark center front, fold line on underlap, end of the opening, buttons and buttonholes with basting.

4 Stitch down the pleat as follows: Stitch from the finished edge of the facing up to the center seam. Leaving in the

6 The photograph shows the finished opening.

2371

Trail blazer

Illustrated Sewing 76

Style 1: This classic three-piece suit combines tartan and plain fabrics. The tartan blazer has smart lapels, large patch pockets, and all edges are top-stitched. Add a straight skirt with an inverted box pleat, then complete the outfit with a plain red waistcoat (**Style 2,** shown in detail overleaf).

Style 3: You can add a plain blazer, this time with a breast pocket as well as the patch pockets and a buttonhole in one lapel. The center back seam ends in a vent for a sporting country flavor.

Style 4: The plaid skirt below and on the right has stitched-down pleats all around.

Styles 1 and 2

2372

Styles 3 and 4

Jackets and blazers never go out of fashion! Here you can choose from a tartan suit or a plain blazer teamed with a pleated plaid skirt. Alternatively, of course, you can mix the jackets and skirts with the rest of your wardrobe. The styles are given in sizes B and D on Pattern Sheet 76.

Style 2: This neat little waistcoat is the perfect complement to the plaid suit. The fronts run to points and there is a small piped pocket with a buttoned tab. The tab detail is repeated on the back with a buckle stitched down with decorative crosses. The waistcoat is fully lined so you can wear it open as well as closed.

Hand-sewn buttonholes

Hand-sewn buttonholes are better for thicker fabrics.

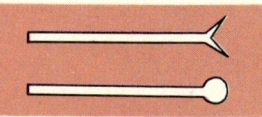

1 Mark the buttonhole on the fabric with a thread, then cut along the marking. Cut diagonally at button end, as shown, at the top, then twist a pencil into this point to make a hole. If you have a punch, punch in a hole first and then cut along the line as shown at the bottom.

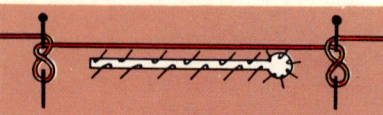

2 Overcast the cut edges to prevent fraying. Then, for added firmness, stretch a heavy thread above the overcasting with two pins as illustrated above.

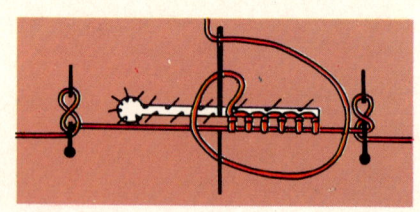

3 When cutting your working thread, make sure it is long enough for the whole buttonhole. Working from right to left, work buttonhole stitch all around, always working over heavy thread. The small knots thus formed must lie close together, just below the edge.

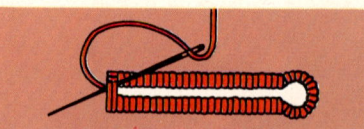

4 At the end, stretch two or three threads across, then wind the thread around them tightly, catching in a few strands of the fabric as you do so.

Lining a garment with self facings

How-to

When making a lining, the basic steps are the same for any garment. Use the garment pattern when cutting out.

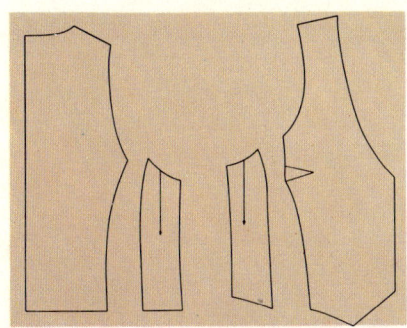

1 Draw the pattern parts onto paper. For this garment, you need the front, side front, side back, and back, as shown above. In most cases, it is the basic pattern parts that are required.

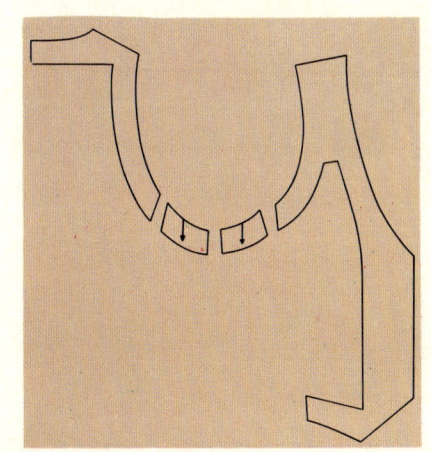

2 Note that the facings of the various pieces are also given. Cut these out in fabric.

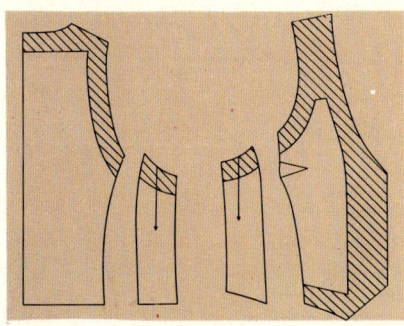

3 For the lining pattern parts, place the facing parts onto the main pattern parts and mark the outlines. For clarity, the facing parts have been shaded and the main parts left plain. The armhole of the back facing has extra width for easing. For this facing, begin by sketching in the upper half, then place the facing to match the side seams exactly. You may have to adjust the lines where they meet.

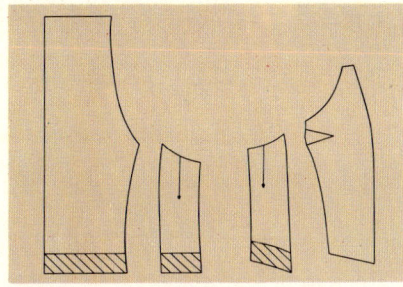

4 On the side and back parts, sketch a line 1 cm ($\frac{3}{8}$") below the hem depth. Cut the lining pieces from lining fabric, adding seam allowance.

5 The photograph above shows the lined garment (the shoulder seams have been left unjoined to show the whole lining).

Iron the interfacings onto the facings and stitch facings together. Stitch the seams of the fabric and then the lining. Stitch the facings to the main pieces, right sides facing, and turn. Press in the hem.

If inserting the lining by machine, begin at the front edge and stitch one seam at a time, working from corner to corner. Secure the ends of the seams, then clip diagonally into the seam allowance close to the last stitch before moving on to the next section. Leave approximately 20 cm (8") open on the hem edge so that the whole garment can be turned to the right side and sewn up by hand. Top-stitch the edges all around to the desired width.

If you prefer to slip-hem the lining into place, turn in the seam allowances on all the edges of the lining, pin into the garment, wrong sides facing and so that seam matches seam. Slip-hem into position.

2375

Sewing

For handlebars and carrier
Easy riders

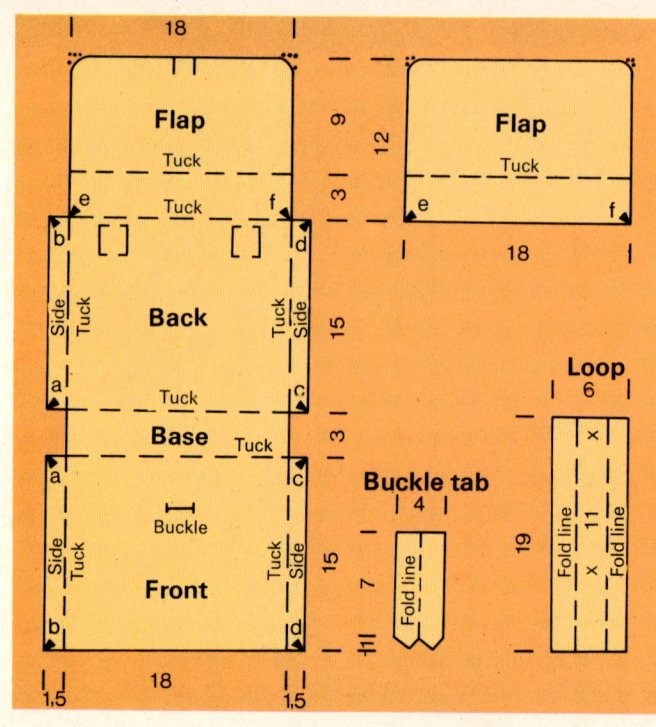

Trying to cycle with a bag dangling precariously from the handlebars or jammed onto the carrier is annoying and can be dangerous if it gets in the way. So make sure the children carry their belongings safely packed away in these ingenious bicycle bags.

Blue saddle bag
Materials Required: Blue sailcloth: 0.70 m ($\frac{3}{4}$ yd), 120 cm (48") wide. White sailcloth: 0.15 m ($\frac{1}{8}$ yd), 120 cm (48") wide. 4 press studs or snaps. Leather needle.

Cutting out: Half of the bag pattern is shown on the blue diagram. Enlarge all pieces to the measurements given. The distance between points **l** and **k** may be adjusted, depending on the width of your luggage rack. Cut out the bag, adding 3 cm ($1\frac{1}{4}$") at the top edge of the fronts and 1 cm ($\frac{3}{8}$") on all other edges. Cut out the pocket flap 4 times with 0.5 cm ($\frac{1}{4}$") seam allowance. Cut out the patch pockets 4 times with a 3 cm ($1\frac{1}{4}$") seam allowance at the upper edge, otherwise 1 cm ($\frac{3}{8}$"). Cut handle to measurements given.

Sewing: Press the seam allowance of the patch pockets to the inside and stitch them on where marked. Finish all cut edges of the bag except for the side seams. Fold in the seam allowance at the top edge of the fronts, snip diagonally into the corners, and stitch down. Along the center of the bag bases, stitch a 0.2 cm ($\frac{1}{16}$") wide pin tuck from the wrong side. Join the side seams, and cutting away any excess fabric, finish the edges together. Join the sides to the base of the bag. Now stitch pin tucks along the marked lines from the right side. Turn under the raw edges along the center section of the bag and top-stitch. Stitch 2 sets of flaps together, snip diagonally across corners, turn, and top-stitch. Finish the edges together along the straight edge. Make a pin

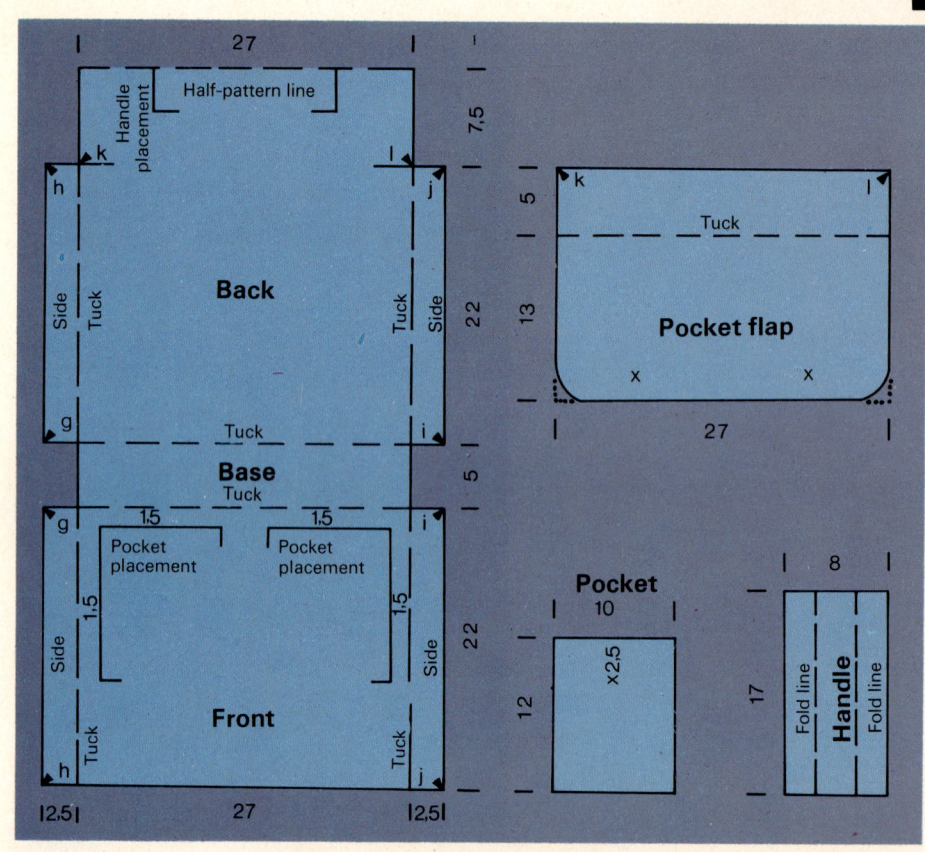

Enlarge the pattern pieces to the measurements given. Numbers are centimeters. Inches are given below.

1 cm = $\frac{3}{8}$"
1.5 cm = $\frac{5}{8}$"
2.5 cm = 1"
3 cm = $1\frac{1}{4}$"
4 cm = $1\frac{5}{8}$"
5 cm = 2"
6 cm = $2\frac{3}{8}$"
7 cm = $2\frac{3}{4}$"
7.5 cm = $2\frac{7}{8}$"
8 cm = $3\frac{1}{8}$"
9 cm = $3\frac{1}{2}$"
10 cm = 4"
12 cm = $4\frac{3}{4}$"
13 cm = $5\frac{1}{8}$"
15 cm = 6"
17 cm = $6\frac{3}{4}$"
18 cm = $7\frac{1}{8}$"
19 cm = $7\frac{1}{2}$"
22 cm = $8\frac{5}{8}$"
27 cm = $10\frac{5}{8}$"

2376

tuck along the marked line from the outside and stitch the flap to the bag, right sides facing and matching points **k** and **l**. Handle: turn in 0.5 cm ($\frac{1}{4}$") seam allowance and fold the strip twice lengthwise so that the edges meet at the center of the underside. Stitch along the handle several times and stitch to the bag where marked. Finally, punch in press studs or snaps where indicated.

Yellow handlebar bag
Materials Required: Sailcloth: 0.30 m ($\frac{3}{8}$ yd), 120 cm (48") wide. 1 buckle without prong. Piece of stiff, transparent plastic for name plate. 2 press studs or snaps. Leather needle.

Cutting out: The whole bag pattern is shown on the yellow diagram. Enlarge it to the measurements given. Cut out the bag with a 1 cm ($\frac{3}{8}$") seam allowance all around, except for the flap which has 0.5 cm ($\frac{1}{4}$"). Cut loops and buckle tab to measurements given.

Sewing: Finish the front top edge and side edges of the base. Stitch the bag flap sections together, snip diagonally across corners, turn, and top-stitch. Stitch the piece of plastic for the name plate onto the flap as shown. Turn in the seam allowance along the front top edge and stitch. Stitch a 0.2 cm ($\frac{1}{16}$") wide pin tuck along the base of the bag from the inside. Join the side seams and, cutting off any excess fabric, finish the edges together. Join the sides to the bag base. Stitch pin tucks along the marked lines from the right side. At the tuck of the self flap, catch in and cut edge of the stitched-on flap. Buckle tab: turn in 0.5 cm ($\frac{1}{4}$") on the long edges and at the point. Fold in half and stitch together close to the edge. Finish the straight edge and stitch to the flap along the top-stitching line. Loops: turn in 0.5 cm ($\frac{1}{4}$") on the narrow sides, then on long sides. Turn under along the fold lines so that the edges meet at the center. Top-stitch. Punch in the press studs or snaps and stitch the loops to the bag with a decorative cross. Finally, sew on the buckle.

This bag fits snugly over the carrier. Pick it up and it becomes a satchel.

The smaller bag loops over the handlebars and can also be worn with a belt. The loops can also be snapped together to form a handle.

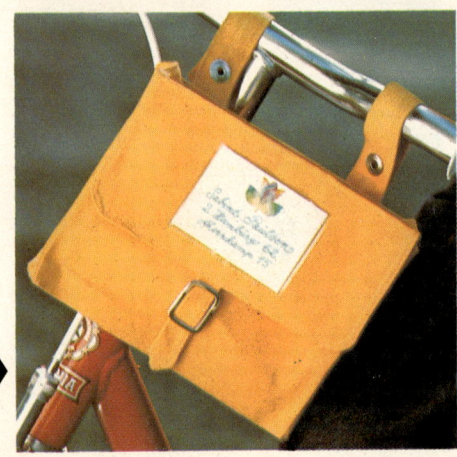

Playing Indians is always a favorite game, so make these colorful costumes for your tribe.

Fringed and feathered

Size: 6–8 year olds, height 116 cm – 128 cm ($45\frac{1}{2}''$ – $50\frac{1}{2}''$). Check lengths first and make any adjustments necessary before cutting out the pattern pieces.

GIRL'S TUNIC

Materials Required: Light brown felt: 0.60 m ($\frac{5}{8}$ yd), 180 cm ($72''$) wide. Dark brown felt: 0.10 m ($\frac{1}{8}$ yd), 180 cm ($72''$) wide. Felt pieces in yellow, red, orange, blue. 1 button. Fabric glue.

Cutting out: Cut out the pieces with 1 cm ($\frac{3}{8}''$) seam allowance, but no allowance at the hem. Fringe: With pinking shears, cut 2 dark brown strips 26 cm x 7 cm ($10\frac{1}{4}''$ x $2\frac{3}{4}''$). Cut fringe to a depth of 5.5 cm ($2\frac{1}{4}''$). Felt strips: Cut these 1 cm ($\frac{3}{8}''$) wide with pinking shears.

Sewing: Glue felt strips to the front neck and sleeves 1 cm ($\frac{3}{8}''$) apart. Join the seams, catching in the fringe on the inner sleeve seams. Turn in the seam allowance at the neck and sleeve hem and stitch. Glue felt strips at the hem. Sew on the button and a loop.

HEAD DRESS

Materials Required: Light brown felt: 0.10 m ($\frac{1}{8}$ yd), 180 cm ($72''$) wide. Heavy non-woven interfacing: 0.10 m ($\frac{1}{8}$ yd), 82 cm ($32''$) wide. Narrow braid: 1.25 m ($1\frac{3}{8}$ yds) each in yellow, red, and blue. Feather. Velcro: 10 cm ($4''$).

Cutting out: Cut 1 strip each of felt and interfacing 55 cm x 9 cm ($21\frac{5}{8}''$ x $3\frac{1}{2}''$).

Sewing: Fold the interfacing in half lengthwise. Baste on the felt and stitch on the braid. Stitch on the Velcro to close the ends.

SANDALS

Materials Required: Felt: 0.10 m ($\frac{1}{8}$ yd), 180 cm ($72''$) wide. Rubber sandals. Fabric glue.

Cutting out: With pinking shears, cut 4 strips 110 cm ($43\frac{1}{2}''$) long, 2 strips 15 cm ($6''$) long, and 2 strips 50 cm ($19\frac{1}{2}''$) long, all 1 cm ($\frac{3}{8}''$) wide.

Glue onto sandals as in the photograph.

BOY'S TUNIC

Materials Required: Light brown felt: 0.60 m ($\frac{5}{8}$ yd), 180 cm ($72''$) wide. Yellow felt: 0.10 m ($\frac{1}{8}$ yd), 180 cm ($72''$) wide. Narrow braid: 4.20 m ($4\frac{5}{8}$ yds) each of yellow, blue, and red. 1 button.

Cutting out: There is no seam allowance at neck and hem, elsewhere 1 cm ($\frac{3}{8}''$). Fringe: With pinking shears, cut 4 strips of each of following lengths: 24 cm, 44 cm, and 29 cm ($9\frac{1}{2}''$, $17\frac{3}{8}''$, and $11\frac{3}{8}''$) by 5 cm ($2''$) wide. Cut fringe to a depth of 4 cm ($1\frac{1}{2}''$). Cut 1 yellow strip 34 cm ($13\frac{1}{2}''$) long and 1 cm ($\frac{3}{8}''$) wide with pinking shears for the neck edge.

Sewing: Stitch braids 0.3 cm ($\frac{1}{8}''$) apart and stitch the fringes on below. Join the seams and press open. Stitch on the felt strip at the neck. Turn under and stitch the sleeve hem. Sew on the button and a loop.

PANTS

Materials Required: Light brown felt: 0.55 m ($\frac{5}{8}$ yd), 180 cm ($72''$) wide. Dark brown felt: 0.10 m ($\frac{1}{8}$ yd), 180 cm ($72''$) wide. Felt pieces in red, orange, yellow. Elastic. Fabric glue.

Cutting out: Cut out twice with a 1 cm ($\frac{3}{8}''$) seam allowance all around. With pinking shears, cut felt strips 45 cm ($17\frac{3}{4}''$) long by 1 cm ($\frac{3}{8}''$) wide. Fringe: With pinking shears, cut 2 strips 62 cm ($24\frac{3}{8}''$) long, 7 cm ($2\frac{3}{4}''$) wide. Cut fringe to a depth of 5 cm ($2''$).

Sewing: Glue on strips at the hem. Join inside leg seam, then crotch seam. Turn in waist seam and draw through elastic. Stitch on the fringe along line marked on pattern.

HEAD DRESS

Materials Required: Felt: 0.10 m ($\frac{1}{8}$ yd), 180 cm ($72''$) wide. Felt pieces in yellow, red, orange. Heavy non-woven interfacing: 0.10 m ($\frac{1}{8}$ yd), 82 cm ($32''$) wide. 13 feathers. Velcro: 10 cm ($4''$).

Cutting out: Cut 1 felt, 1 interfacing strip 55 cm x 9 cm ($21\frac{1}{2}''$ x $3\frac{1}{2}''$). Cut felt strips 1 cm ($\frac{3}{8}''$) wide.

Sewing: Fold interfacing in half lengthwise, baste the felt around it and sew on the feathers 4 cm ($1\frac{1}{2}''$) apart. Stitch on the felt strips. At the ends, stitch on Velcro.

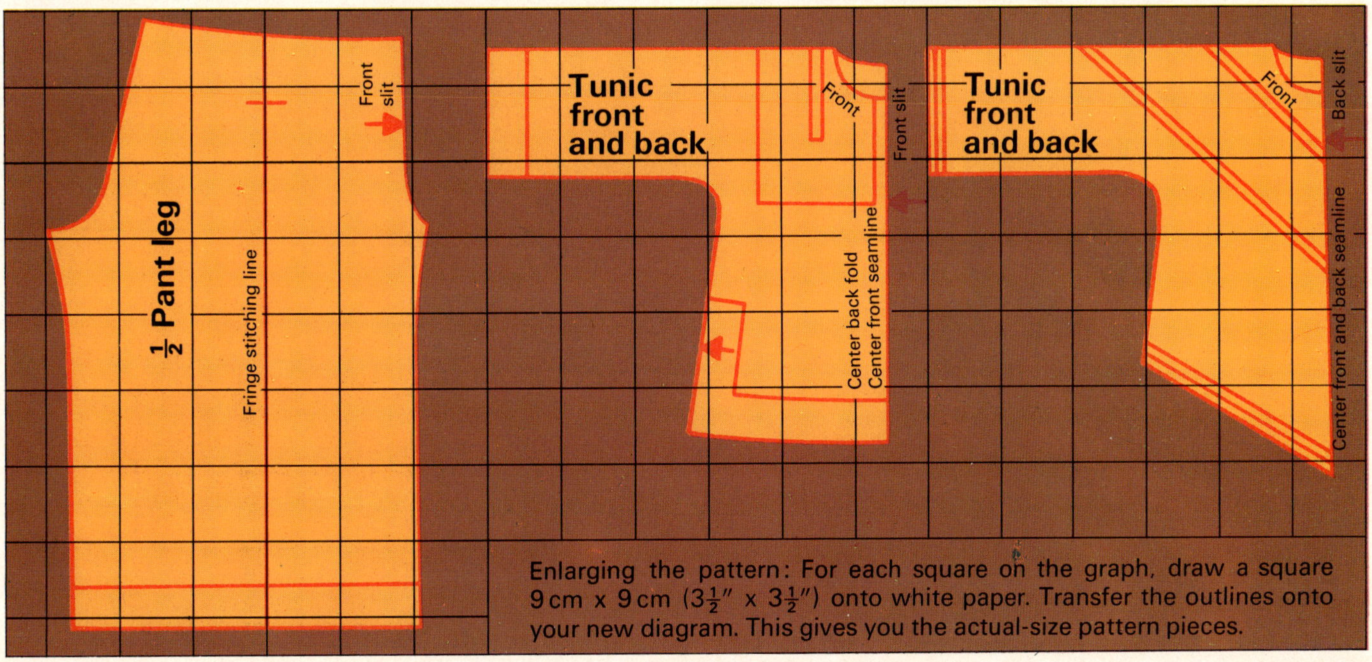

Enlarging the pattern: For each square on the graph, draw a square 9 cm x 9 cm ($3\frac{1}{2}''$ x $3\frac{1}{2}''$) onto white paper. Transfer the outlines onto your new diagram. This gives you the actual-size pattern pieces.

Materials Required: The puppets' bodies are made from remnants of fake-fur fabric (for colors, see photograph), with cotton fabric or felt for the mouth, tongue, and ears. Glass eyes have been used for the donkey, cow, and monkey, while, for the frog and crocodile, buttons are very effective (sew a round button over a flat button as illustrated). You will also require a small amount of grey yarn for the donkey's mane and a piece of rickrack braid for the crocodile's teeth. For the stuffing for the head, use batting or wadding, or foam chips.

Cutting out: The pieces for the animal heads are given on Pattern Sheet 74, as well as the front and back body parts which are the same for all animals.

Seam allowances: Add 1 cm ($\frac{3}{8}$") seam allowance and 2 cm ($\frac{3}{4}$") at hem. Cut out the appropriate head pieces for each animal; cut out the mouth part twice. For the cow and donkey, cut out the tongue twice.

Sewing: For the monkey and donkey, stitch and turn the ears first. For the cow, stitch and turn the ears and horns. The following instructions apply to all animals.

Pin back of head to back, right sides facing. Then pin the inner lining to back of head,

You must hand it to them

Hand puppets are an excellent way of stimulating children's imagination. Our set of cheerful animal glove puppets will give them hours of entertainment, and you too! The pattern pieces are given actual size on Pattern Sheet 74.

wrong sides facing (this will encase the stuffing). Stitch these pieces together from corner to corner through all layers, but do not stitch into the seam allowance on either side. Stitch the other relevant face pieces together, matching letters.
For monkey, donkey and cow, baste the ears (and horns) to the back of head where marked. Stitch the finished face to the curve of back of head, right sides facing. Turn and stuff the head.
Stitch and turn tongue for cow and donkey. Join the center seam of mouth pieces, catching in tongue for cow and donkey.

With wrong sides facing, pin the inner lining fabric (which encloses the stuffed head) to the upper lip. Place the mouth along the same line, right sides facing, and stitch through all layers from corner to corner, catching in rickrack braid for the crocodile. Stitch lower jaw to front body, right sides facing. Stitch the mouth to the lower jaw right sides facing.
Stitch the front and back body together at the sides, right sides facing. Turn up the hem at the lower edge and stitch. Turn the puppet to the right side. Finally sew on the eyes securely.

2381

For a comfortable life

RUG

Keeping economy in mind, make the rug with strips of fabric scraps or buy remnants of cheap cotton from department stores. You can vary the size of the rug, but remember that the length will decrease slightly when you work the lines of quilting.

Size: Approximately 120 cm x 235 cm (47$\frac{1}{4}$" x 92$\frac{1}{2}$").

Materials Required: Fabric: For top of rug: various cotton fabrics, plain and printed; for rug backing: plain fabric 2.45 m (2$\frac{3}{4}$ yds), 150 cm (60") wide. Strips of fabric for binding the edges: 2 strips 120 cm (47$\frac{1}{4}$") long and 2 strips 245 cm (96$\frac{1}{2}$") long, each 8 cm (3") wide. Batting or wadding for interlining: 2.45 m (2$\frac{3}{4}$ yds), 150 cm (60") wide.

Making the rug

Cut out one layer of interlining and one piece of backing fabric to the overall measurements for the rug. Sort out the various fabrics for the top of the rug according to pattern and color. In all, cut out 22 strips, following the measurements on the diagram and adding 1 cm ($\frac{3}{8}$") seam allowance to the long sides. Stitch these strips together and press seam to one side.

Sandwich the layer of interlining between the top fabric and the backing, wrong sides facing and open-edged. Baste through all layers of fabric around the edge of the rug and along each strip. Stitch through the seamlines of all strips.

Bind the shorter sides of the rug with the relevant strips as follows: With 1 cm ($\frac{3}{8}$") seam allowance, stitch the strips to the rug, right sides facing, 3 cm (1$\frac{1}{8}$") from the edge. Fold the binding over to the back, turn in seam allowance; sew down. Work long sides in same way.

CUSHIONS

Cushion 1: Cut out 2 pieces of plain cotton in overall measurements shown in diagram with 1 cm ($\frac{3}{8}$") seam allowance all around. For filling, cut 5 layers of batting or wadding to same dimensions, but without seam allowance. Baste a layer of filling against wrong side of cushion front. Stitch along vertical stitching lines (see diagram).

Cushion 2: Following measurements on diagram, cut out one piece of plain fabric for cushion back and several strips for cushion front with 1 cm ($\frac{3}{8}$") seam allowance all around. For filling, cut 5 layers of batting or wadding without seam allowance. Stitch the fabric strips together and press seams to one side. Baste a layer of filling against the wrong side and stitch through the seamlines.

Cushion 3: Following measurements on diagram, cut out 1 piece each of plain and printed cotton with 1 cm ($\frac{3}{8}$") seam allowance all around. For filling: cut 5 layers of batting or wadding without seam allowance. Baste a layer of filling against cushion front and stitch along horizontal stitching lines.

Cushion 4: For cushion back, cut out one piece of plain cotton in given measurements with 1 cm ($\frac{3}{8}$") seam allowance all around. For front border, cut 4 strips in plain cotton each 40 cm (15$\frac{3}{4}$") long and 5 cm (2") wide with 1 cm ($\frac{3}{8}$") seam allowance all around. For center, cut one square in plain cotton and one printed strip according to measurements on diagram, plus 1 cm ($\frac{3}{8}$") seam allowance. For filling, cut 5 layers of batting or wadding without seam allowance. Miter corners of 4 edge strips. Press under seam allowances of the long sides of printed strip and stitch strip onto center square as shown in diagram. Press under seam allowance of the square and stitch onto the border. Baste a layer of filling to wrong side and stitch through the seamlines.

Cushion 5: Following diagram, cut out 2 pieces of plain cotton with 1 cm ($\frac{3}{8}$") seam allowance all around and 5 layers of batting or wadding without seam allowance for filling. Baste the top piece of fabric to a layer of filling and stitch the pattern of squares as shown on diagram.

Finishing: Stitch all covers together and turn, leaving opening for filling. Fill and sew up opening by hand.

◀ **Diagram:** Cut out the fabric and interlining to the measurements shown. Numbers are centimeters; inch equivalents are given.

Inch equivalents: 1 cm = $\frac{3}{8}$"; 3 cm = 1$\frac{1}{8}$"; 4 cm = 1$\frac{5}{8}$"; 4.5 cm = 1$\frac{7}{8}$"; 5 cm = 2"; 7 cm = 2$\frac{7}{8}$"; 8 cm = 3$\frac{1}{8}$"; 8.5 cm = 3$\frac{3}{8}$"; 9 cm = 3$\frac{1}{2}$"; 10 cm = 3$\frac{7}{8}$"; 11 cm = 4$\frac{3}{8}$"; 12.5 cm = 5"; 13 cm = 5$\frac{1}{8}$"; 14 cm = 5$\frac{1}{2}$"; 15.5 cm = 6$\frac{1}{8}$"; 16 cm = 6$\frac{1}{4}$"; 16.5 cm = 6$\frac{1}{2}$"; 17 cm = 6$\frac{5}{8}$"; 18 cm = 7$\frac{1}{8}$"; 18.5 cm = 7$\frac{3}{8}$"; 20 cm = 7$\frac{7}{8}$"; 21 cm = 8$\frac{1}{4}$"; 30 cm = 11$\frac{3}{4}$"; 40 cm = 15$\frac{3}{4}$"; 120 cm = 47$\frac{1}{4}$"; 243 cm = 95$\frac{5}{8}$".

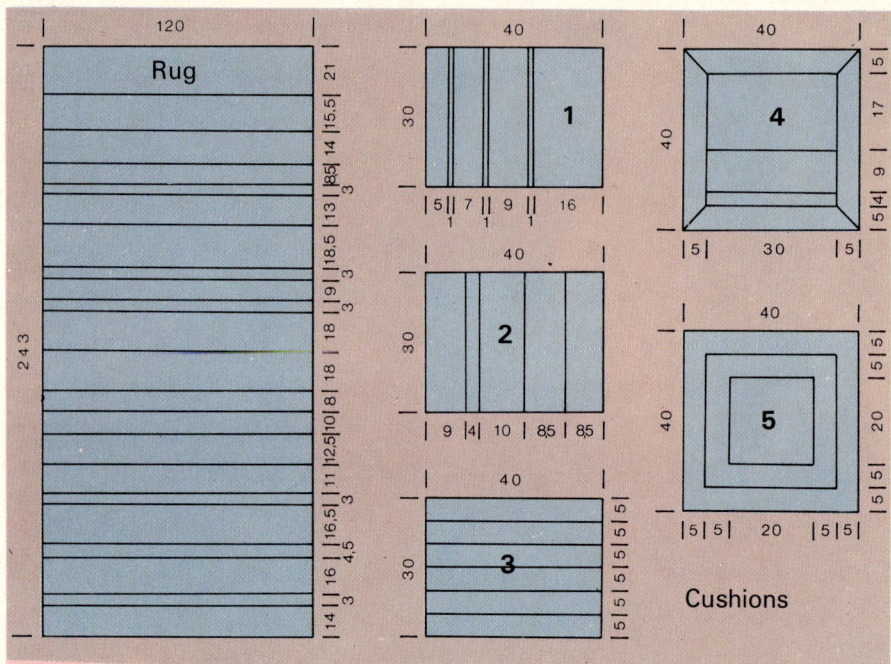

Here's a soft, quilted rug for any room which needs a little color and warmth. It's made of strips of cotton. Any extra fabric can be used for matching cushions.

A square deal

Make a patchwork quilt with a difference by padding each square separately. It will then be warm as well as decorative. Use checked fabrics as shown here or a selection of floral prints.

Size: The quilt illustrated, inclusive of ruffle, measures 0.90 m (35½") wide and 1.80 m (71") long. You can make it in any size, but bear in mind that the squares lose about 2 cm (¾") in width and length by filling.

Materials Required: Selection of checked cottons for quilt top (you will need 36 squares; see diagram for measurements). Checked cotton: 1.85 m (2 yds), 90 cm (36") wide for underside; 1.60 m (1¾ yds), 90 cm (36") wide for ruffle. Batting or wadding for interlining: 3.30 m (3⅝ yds), 150 cm (58") wide.

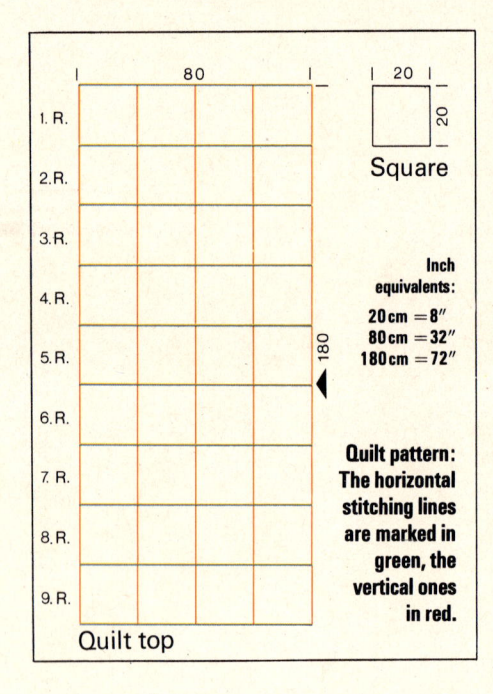

Quilt pattern: The horizontal stitching lines are marked in green, the vertical ones in red.

Inch equivalents:
20 cm = 8"
80 cm = 32"
180 cm = 72"

Quilt top

Making the quilt

For underside of quilt, cut a piece 80 cm x 180 cm (32" x 72"), plus 1 cm (⅜") seam allowance all around. For the ruffle, cut strips measuring 11 m (12 yds) long in all by 10 cm (4") wide, plus 1 cm (⅜") seam allowance all around.

For quilt top, make a square cardboard template 20 cm x 20 cm (8" x 8"). Cut out 36 squares from checked fabric, adding 1 cm (⅜") seam allowance all around.

Again using the template, cut out 108 squares in interlining without seam allowance. (You will need 3 squares of interlining to fill each square of fabric).

Sort out the fabric squares according to design and color and plan the arrangement. Stitch together 4 squares at a time, and press seam allowances to one side. Stitch the separate strips together. Press the seams as before. Place the top and underside of the quilt together, wrong sides facing. Baste both layers of fabric together on the long sides. First stitch one center horizontal line (see green line marked with arrow on diagram). Then stitch all vertical lines (see red lines on diagram). Fill the center row of 4 squares with the interlining, then close these squares by stitching the quilt together along the next horizontal line (see next green line on diagram). Baste, stitch, and fill the remaining squares in the same way, working from the center to end in one direction, then from the center to the other end.

Stitch the ruffle strips together and join to a circle. Press the seam allowance under twice along one long side and stitch down. Gather the other side to the required length. Stitch the ruffle, right sides facing, to the top and finish the seams together. Fold ruffle down and top-stitch close to edge.

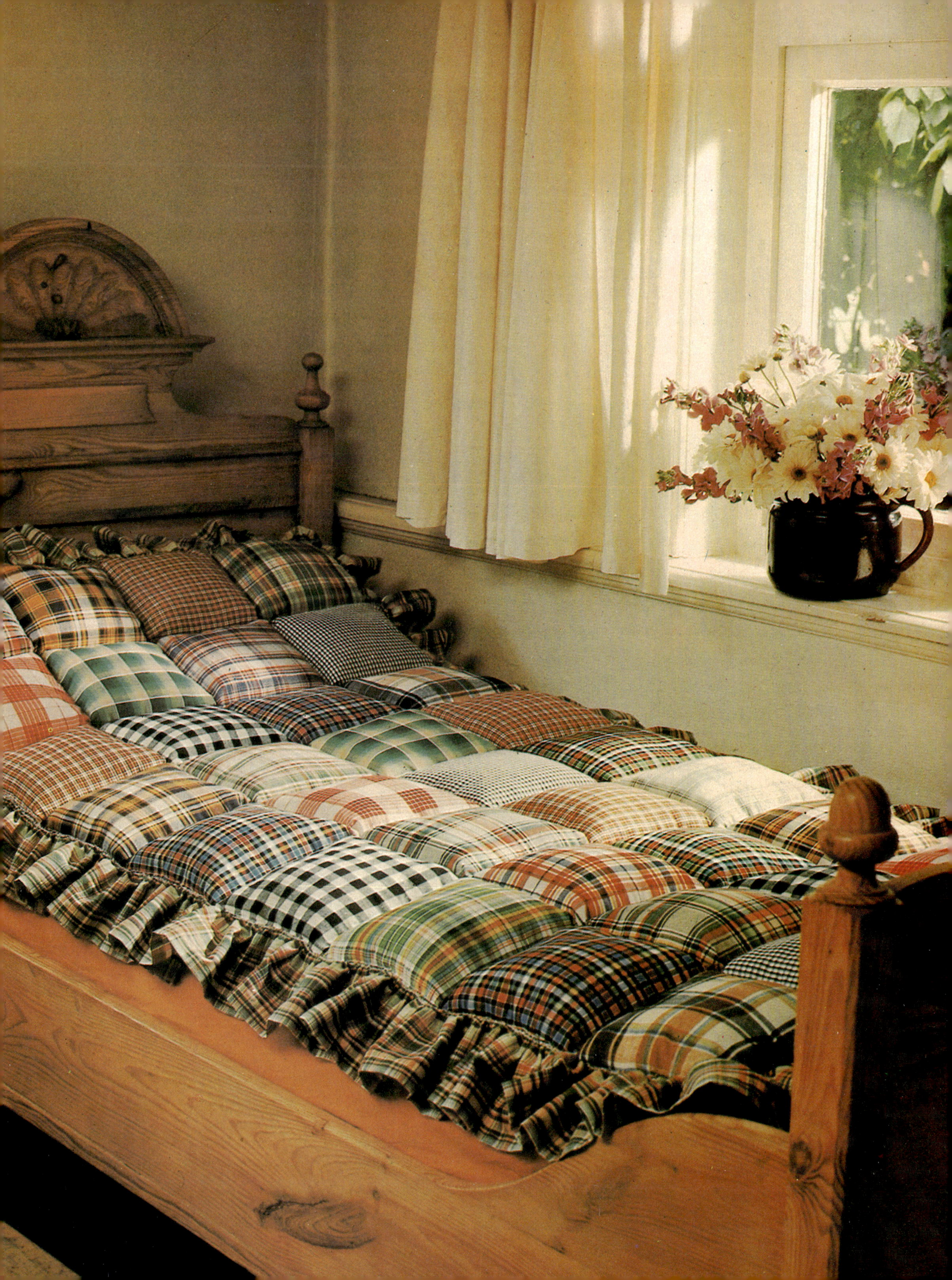

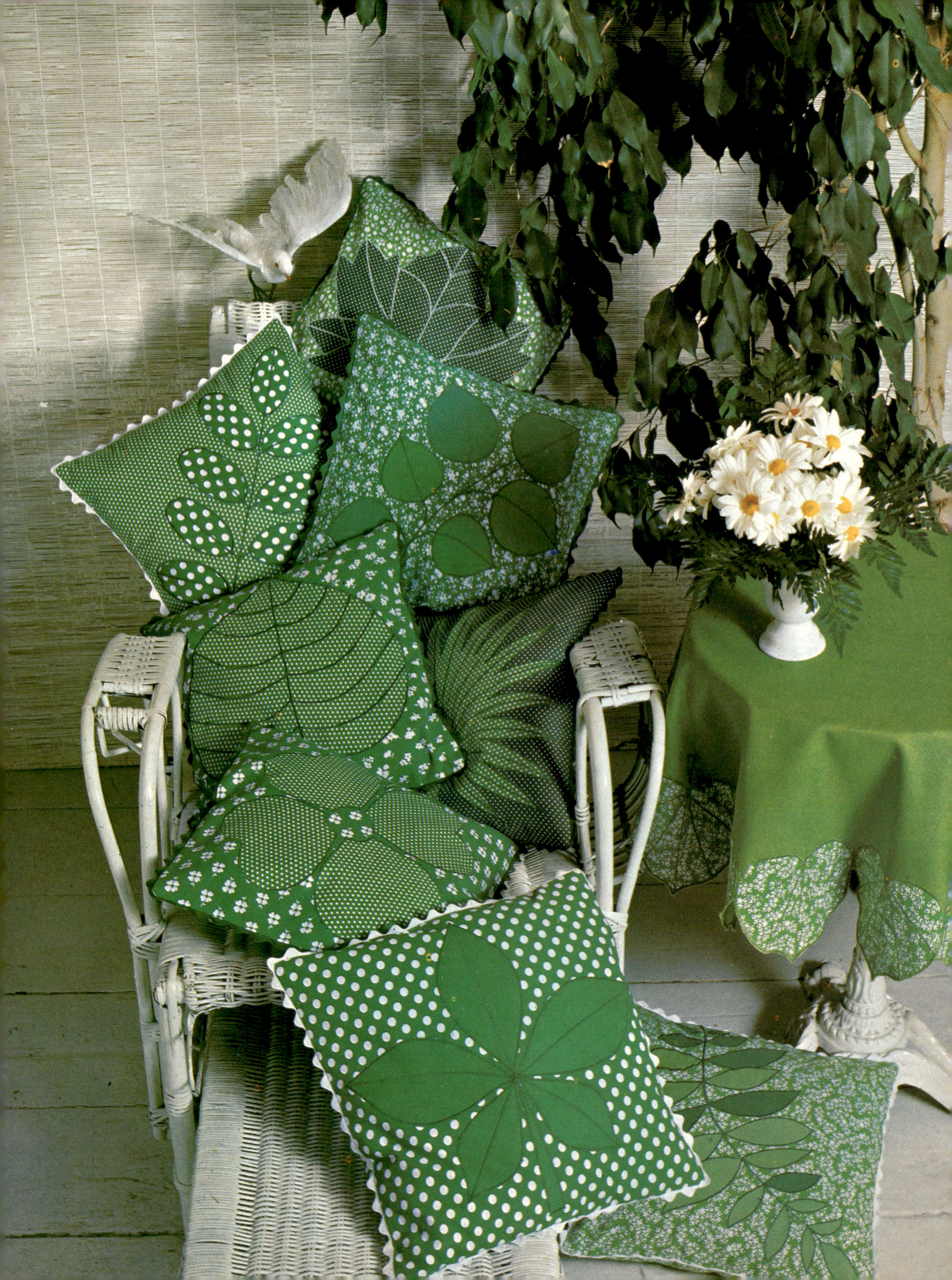

Green leaves of summer

Bring the freshness of the countryside into your home with our leafy cushion collection. Choose a variety of printed and plain cottons in green and white. There is an appliqué tablecloth to match.

Size: The cushions are 40 cm (15¾") square. The round tablecloth has a diameter of 1.10 m (43½").

Materials Required:

Cushions: Printed cotton for one cushion cover: 0.45 m (½ yd), 90 cm (36") wide. Remnant of cotton for appliqué. Wide rickrack braid: 1.65 m (1⅞ yds). Kapok or foam chips for filling.

Tablecloth: Cotton fabric: 1.10 m (1¼ yds), 115 cm (45") wide. Printed cotton for appliqués: 0.70 m (¾ yd), 90 cm (36") wide.

Working the designs

The designs are given actual size on the front of Pattern Sheet 76. Some of the leaf sprays are complete, others can be built up from the parts given. You can also make up your own leaf designs, using real leaves as inspiration and drawing them in a simplified form. Books too, especially reference books, are a good source of ideas.

Cushion: For 1 cushion, cut 2 squares measuring 40 cm x 40 cm (15¾" x 15¾") with 1 cm (⅜") seam allowance all around. The cushion front is appliquéd first. Cut out the desired leaf shapes from the remnant of cotton and arrange onto the front square (use the photograph as a guide). Baste on the appliqué pieces. Draw in leaf veins and stems with a soft pencil. First stitch these lines, then the leaf outlines with close zigzag stitching. Stitch on the rickrack braid all around, 1 cm (⅜") from the cut edge. Stitch the front and back of the cushion together, right

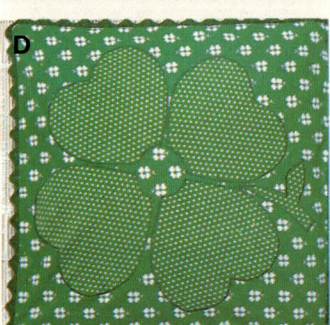

◀ Leaf shapes A to F are given actual size on Pattern Sheet 76. You can also design other leaf shapes yourself.

2387

sides facing and leaving an opening for the filling. Turn to the right side. Finally, fill the cushion and sew up opening by hand.

Tablecloth: Spread out the fabric on the floor. Mark the center of the cloth with a cross of basting stitches. Describe a circle from this point [radius 55 cm (21$\frac{5}{8}$"), diameter 110 cm (43$\frac{1}{2}$")]. An easy way to do this is to make a loop in a piece of string and place a pencil into the loop. Measuring from the pencil, mark off the radius on the string. Holding the mark on the string at the center of the cloth, draw the circle.

From the printed fabric, cut 17 leaf shapes (Pattern Sheet 76, design G) without seam allowance. Arrange these on the cloth so that the cut edges of the leaves meet and the points of the leaves are on the curve of the circle. Baste the leaf shapes to the cloth. Draw in the veins and a stem with a soft pencil.

Stitch precisely around the leaf outlines with close zigzag stitching, then stitch the veins and stem. Finally, cut away the remaining fabric around the tablecloth edge, cutting close to the zigzag outlines.

A detail of the tablecloth shows the appliquéd leaves. The leaf veins and stems are also worked in close zigzag stitch.

Rose of rosettes

Here is a way of using up your colored scraps for an unusual patchwork effect. These blossoms are made of gathered circles of fabric sewn onto a background fabric. Use oddments with a small pattern, either all the same design in lots of different colors (like the round cushion) or various patterns — stripes, checks, plain, flowered — arranged in rows according to color (like the square cushion). If you haven't got enough matching scraps, a complete mixture of colors can be just as effective (rectangular cushion).

Making the cushions
For the blossoms, cut the scraps of fabric into circles with a 6 cm (2½") radius. Turn about 0.5 cm (¼") to the wrong side and draw a gathering thread through all around with small stitches. Pull the thread up tight, fasten off.
Make the cushion cover from matching fabric or buy a ready-made cushion. Our cushions are in the following sizes: Rectangular: 45 cm x 55 cm (17¾" x 21½"). Square: 40 cm x 40 cm (15¾" x 15¾"). Round: 45 cm (17¾") diameter. Before cutting out the cover fabric, place the blossoms in position to make sure they fit, as the diameter may alter according to how tightly they are gathered. Cut out the cover with a 1 cm (⅜") seam allowance. Pin the blossoms flat onto the cover (except for the outer rows) before making it up. Sew them together, at the same time stitch them to the fabric of the cover.
Then stitch around 3 sides of the cover, leaving the fourth side open for turning. Turn to the right side and then sew on the outer rows of blossoms, so that they are not caught into the stitching. Insert cushion and sew 4th side closed. Insert a zipper if desired.

Folklore revival

Brighten up your day with a richly-embroidered peasant blouse that looks especially charming with a long, gathered skirt. We give the pattern for the blouse and embroidery motifs.

Size: 80 cm (31½") or 88 cm (34½") bust.

Materials Required: (for both sizes) For sewing: Cotton batiste: 2.20 m (2⅜ yds), 90 cm (36") wide. 2 buttons. Narrow ribbon or cord: 1 m (1 yd).

For embroidery: Stranded cotton: 4 skeins red; 3 skeins green; 2 skeins each pink, pale blue, dark blue, turquoise, yellow. Organza: 50 cm (½ yd). Embroidery hoop.

Basic Stitches: French knots, backstitch, satin stitch, stem stitch, lazy daisy stitch, four-sided stitch, cross-stitch.

Preparing the fabric: Enlarge the blouse pattern to the correct size from the graph. Tape pieces together at the shoulder and pin to the fabric. Outline the shape with small running stitches in sewing cotton. Do not cut out exactly until the embroidery is complete, to avoid fraying.

Embroidery: Transfer the design onto the fabric with dressmaker's carbon paper. Position the front bands 1 cm ($\frac{3}{8}''$) from center front and the neck bands 1.5 cm ($\frac{5}{8}''$) from the neck edge. Half the sleeve band is given. Transfer it to the sleeve where indicated. Baste organza under all parts to be embroidered.

Work the curved and straight outlines in backstitch, using 4 strands of cotton. Use 2 strands for all the other motifs.

The squares are worked in four-sided stitch filled in with a cross-stitch; the flowers are in satin stitch with backstitch stems. Work the large teardrop shapes in stem stitch at the pointed end, in diagonal satin stitch at the thicker, rounded end, fill them in with lazy daisy stitch. The small teardrops are lazy daisy stitches; the dots are French knots. Follow the photograph opposite for the colors.

Cutting out: Seam allowances: at the neck edge, add 0.5 cm ($\frac{1}{4}''$); at the front edge, add 3.5 cm ($1\frac{3}{8}''$) for the length of the slit; for the hem, add 2 cm ($\frac{3}{4}''$); elsewhere, add 1 cm ($\frac{3}{8}''$).

For the cuffs, cut 2 strips each 19 cm ($7\frac{1}{2}''$) long and 6 cm ($2\frac{1}{4}''$) wide, plus seam allowance. For the sleeve slit, cut 2 strips each 18 cm x 2 cm ($7\frac{1}{8}''$ x $\frac{3}{4}''$). The neck edge is finished with a bias strip about 40 cm ($15\frac{3}{4}''$) long by 3 cm ($1\frac{1}{4}''$) wide.

Sewing: Stitch the side and sleeve seams in one continuous seam, then stitch the center back seam and the center front up to the slit opening. Snip diagonally into the front seam allowance at the last stitch. Press the fabric along the slit at center front to the inside along the seamline. Press under the raw edge 1 cm ($\frac{3}{8}''$).

Press the bias neck strip along the center lengthwise, shaping it as you press. Stitch both thicknesses to the neck edge, right sides facing, turning in the ends at the front. Then turn to the wrong side and stitch to make a 0.5 cm ($\frac{1}{4}''$) wide casing for the ribbon.

Finish all raw edges together close to the seam, and only then cut off the excess fabric. Sew the seam allowance along the slit to the embroidery by hand. Turn the hem under twice and stitch. Sleeve slit: cut along the marked line. Stitch the right side of the strip to the wrong side of the slit, 0.5 cm ($\frac{1}{4}''$) from the edge (tailing off at the upper end). Turn the strip to the right side, turn in the raw edge 0.5 cm ($\frac{1}{4}''$), and stitch down along previous seam. Stitch the upper corner of the strip together diagonally to prevent it from turning to the outside. Gather the lower edge of the sleeve to 18 cm ($7\frac{1}{8}''$). Reinforce the cuff to 1 cm ($\frac{3}{8}''$) beyond the fold line with batiste or soft interfacing. Sew on the cuff with a 1 cm ($\frac{3}{8}''$) underlap and top-stitch all around. Make buttonholes and sew on the buttons.

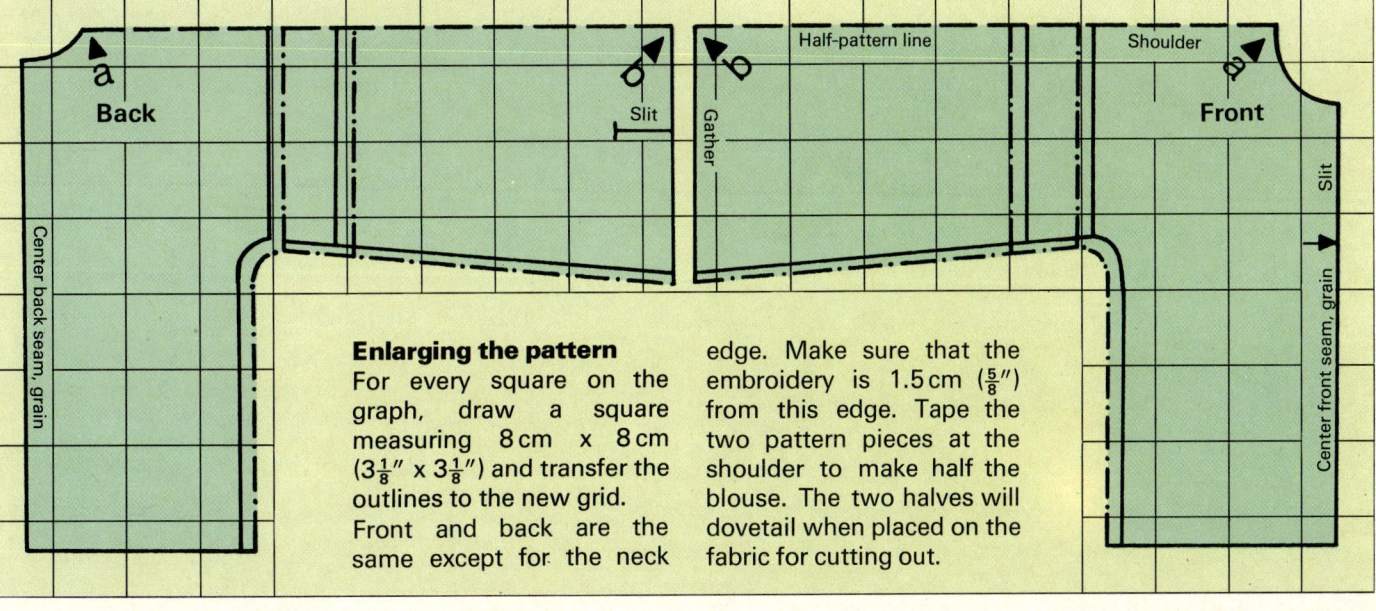

Enlarging the pattern
For every square on the graph, draw a square measuring 8 cm x 8 cm ($3\frac{1}{8}''$ x $3\frac{1}{8}''$) and transfer the outlines to the new grid.

Front and back are the same except for the neck edge. Make sure that the embroidery is 1.5 cm ($\frac{5}{8}''$) from this edge. Tape the two pattern pieces at the shoulder to make half the blouse. The two halves will dovetail when placed on the fabric for cutting out.

Peasant style

The trace patterns on the following pages are for the neck and sleeve bands of the embroidered peasant blouse. Join the sections by matching up the letters as indicated.

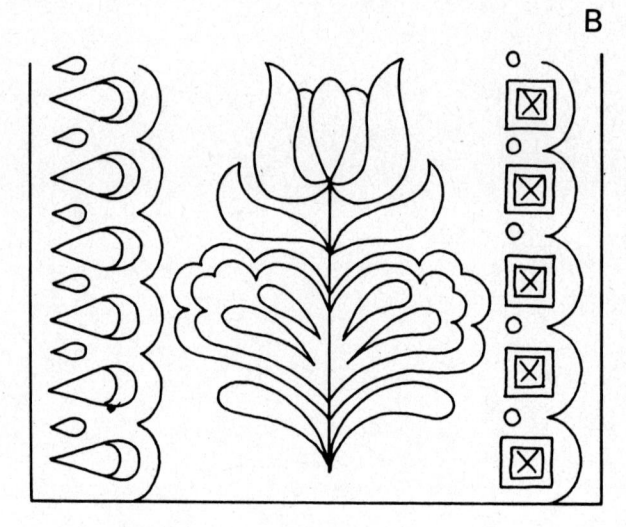

Base of right front neck motif

A

B

Base of left front neck motif

½ sleeve motif

Left back neck motif

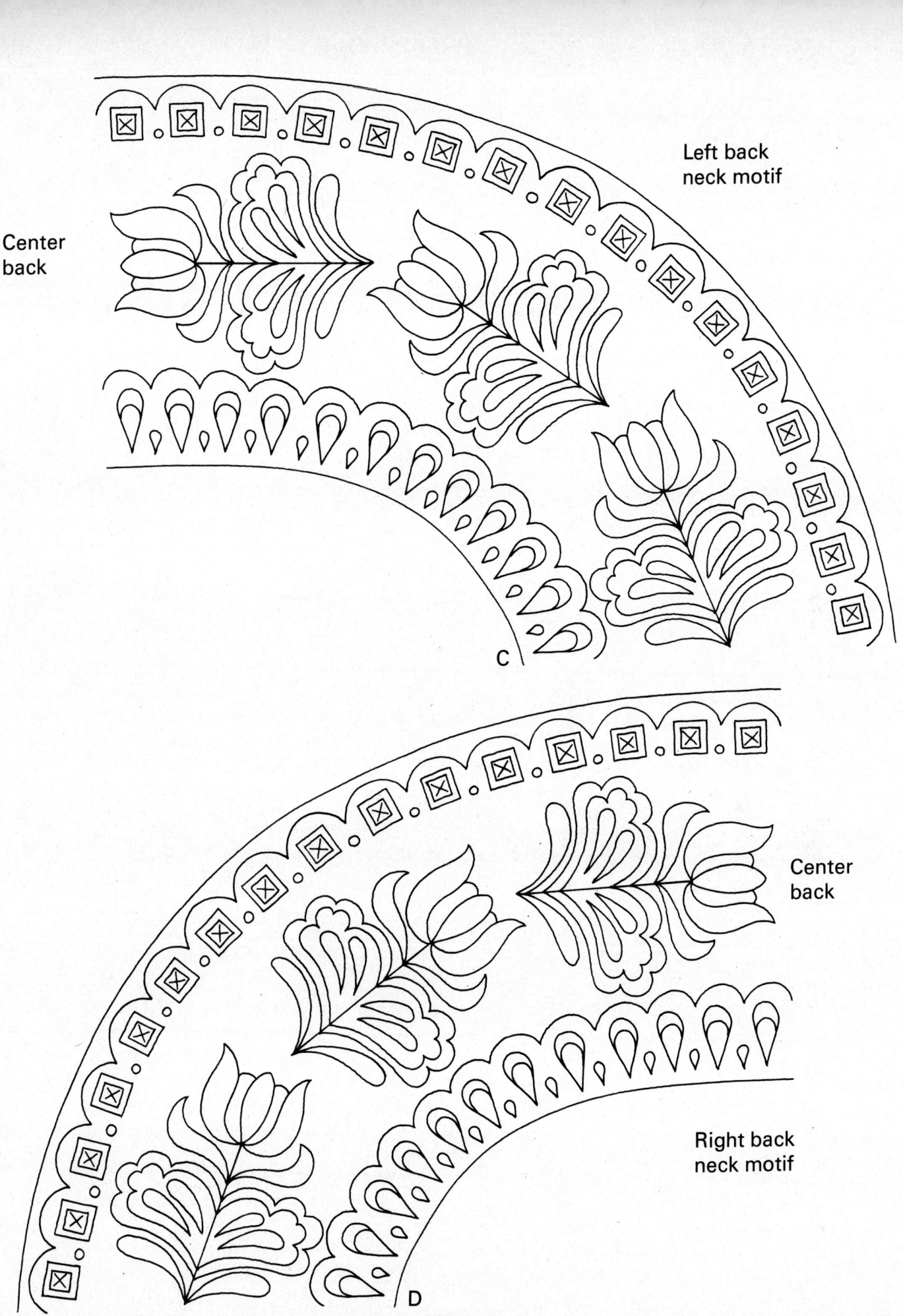

Center back

C

Center back

Right back neck motif

D

2393

Join D here

Right front
neck motif

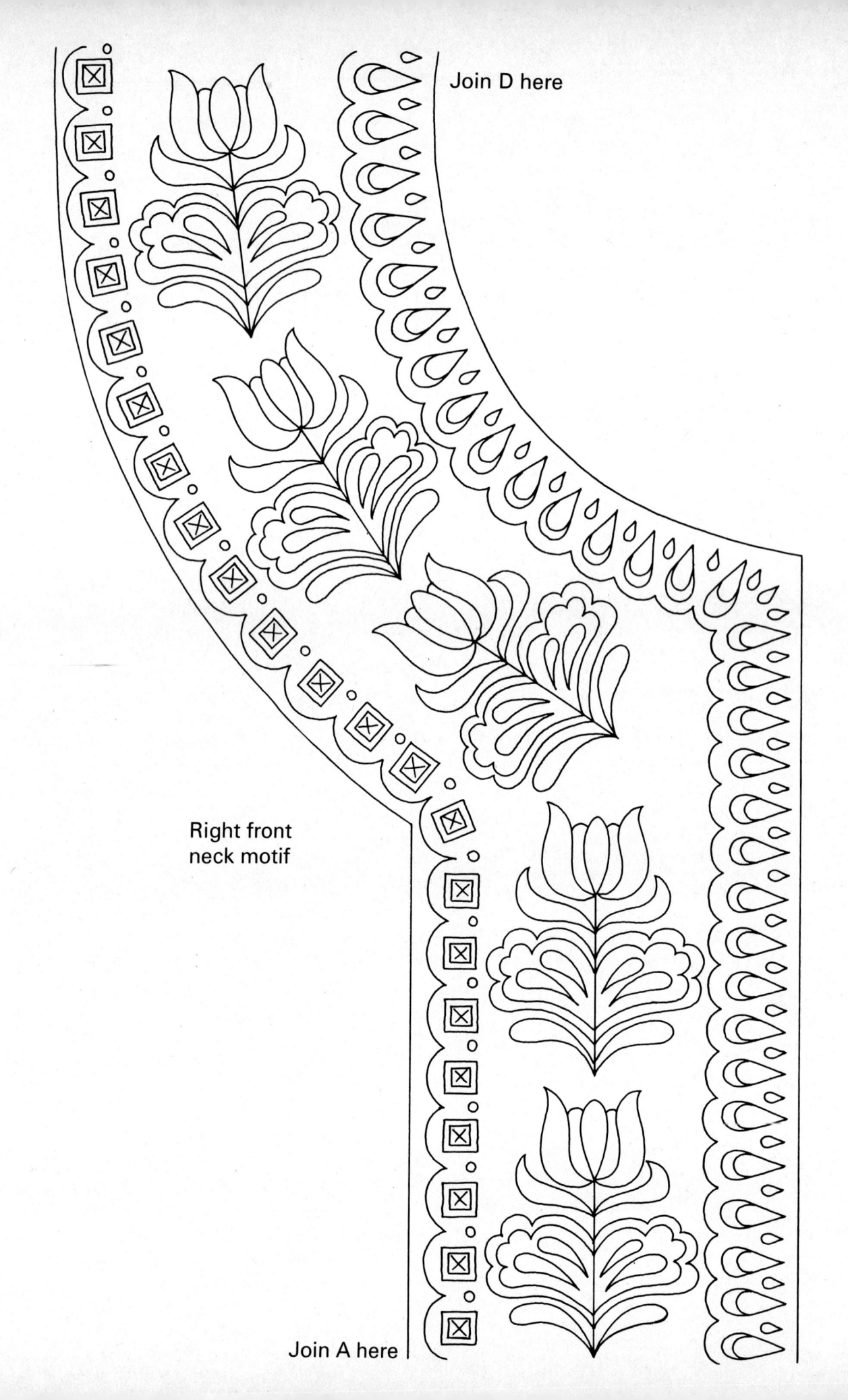

2394 Join A here

Join C here

Left front neck motif

Join B here

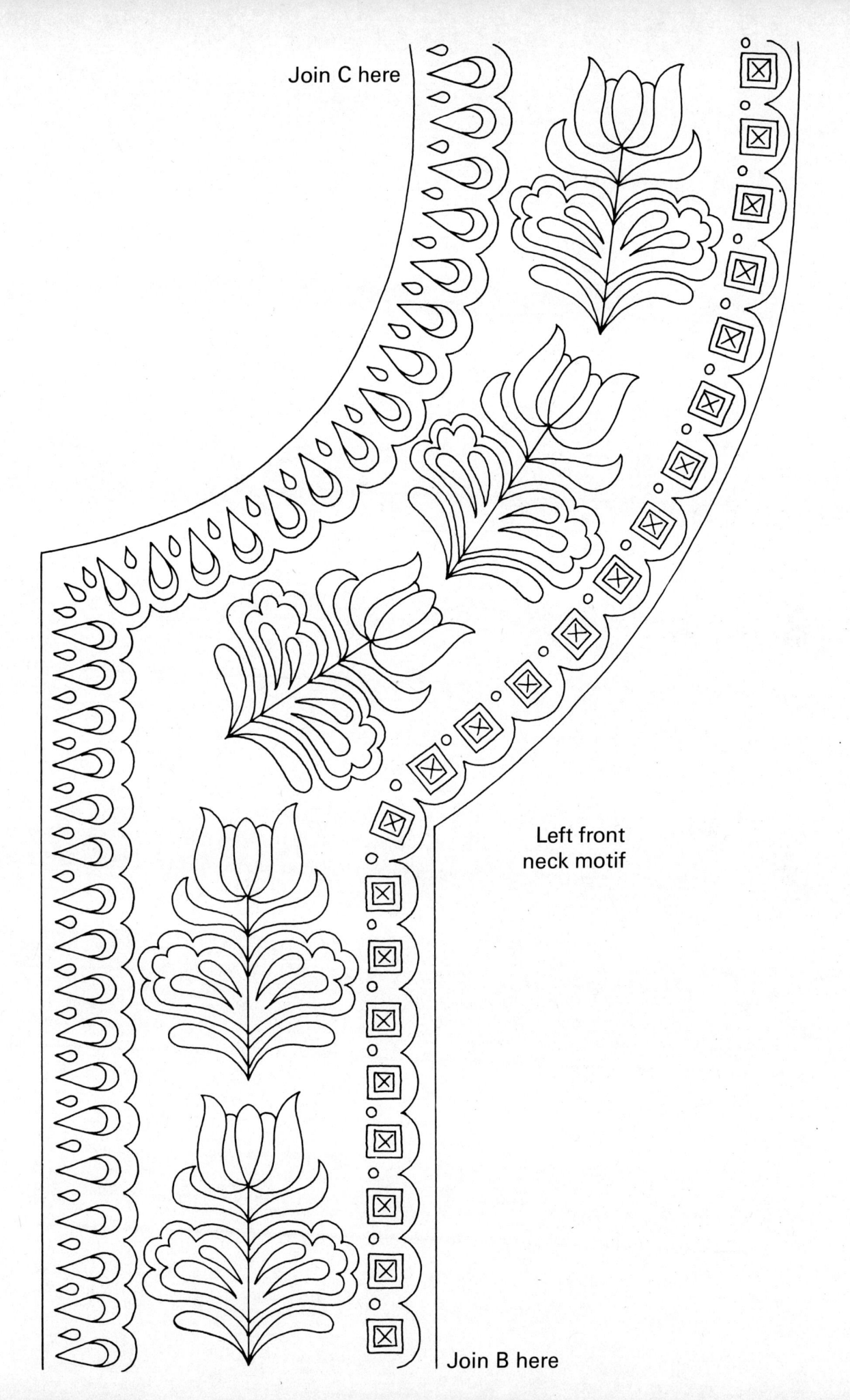

2395

Pride and glory

For the adventurous needlewoman, this masterpiece of a tablecloth offers a challenging, but satisfying project.

We have adapted this design so that you can embroider it yourself from the chart below.
A perfect result depends on careful counting.

Size: Approximately 137 cm x 109 cm (54" x 43").

Materials Required: Stranded embroidery cotton: 10 skeins pink, 8 skeins beige, 7 skeins green, 5 skeins each red and grey, 3 skeins each black, dark blue and blue, 2 skeins each pale green and pale blue, 1 skein yellow. White even-weave fabric, 9 threads to 1 cm (24 threads to 1"): 1.80 m

(2 yds), 150 cm (59") wide.

Basic Stitch: Cross-stitch over 2 threads of weave each way, using half the strands of cotton.

Making the cloth

Trim the fabric to measure exactly 150 cm x 180 cm (59" x 72"). Work the Wide Border first, followed by the Upper and Lower Edge Motifs, then the Narrow Border, and the Stars.

To place the Wide Border, first mark the center of one long side, 15 cm (6") away from the edge of the fabric. Begin at the center mark with the center of the Flower Motif (at left-hand side of chart). Work the Half Repeat, including the center of the Basket Motif, then complete the other half of the Flower Motif on the other side of the center mark by following the chart in reverse without the 2 motif centers (126 crosses). Finish the right half of the side by working one more complete repeat and the Half Corner Motif. Finish the left half by working one more complete repeat and the Half Corner Motif in reverse. Continue to work around the cloth from right to left. Embroider the short sides with the Half Corner Motif, two complete repeats, and the Half Corner Motif in reverse. Embroider the other long side with the Half Corner Motif, three complete repeats, and the Half Corner Motif in reverse. Now embroider Upper and Lower Edge Motifs; begin at one corner and work around in one direction.

Then work the Narrow Border 56 threads up from the Upper Edge Motif on the long sides and 54 threads up on the short sides. On each side, begin centrally and at the center of a repeat pattern.

Finally work the Stars. For this, mark the exact center of the tablecloth with basting thread and work the first Star here. Continue in a lengthwise direction as follows: work another 4 Stars on each side of the center Star with 46 threads between each Star, i.e. 9 Stars in all. To left and right of this center row, work another two rows of Stars each side, each 46 threads apart, i.e. 5 rows in all. Then, between these, work more Star rows of 10 Stars each in a staggered formation. Work the Stars in a variety of colors such as dark blue with beige cross and red center or grey with pink cross and red center.

Finally, trim any excess fabric to give a 9 cm (3½") border all around, and turn in a small hem twice.

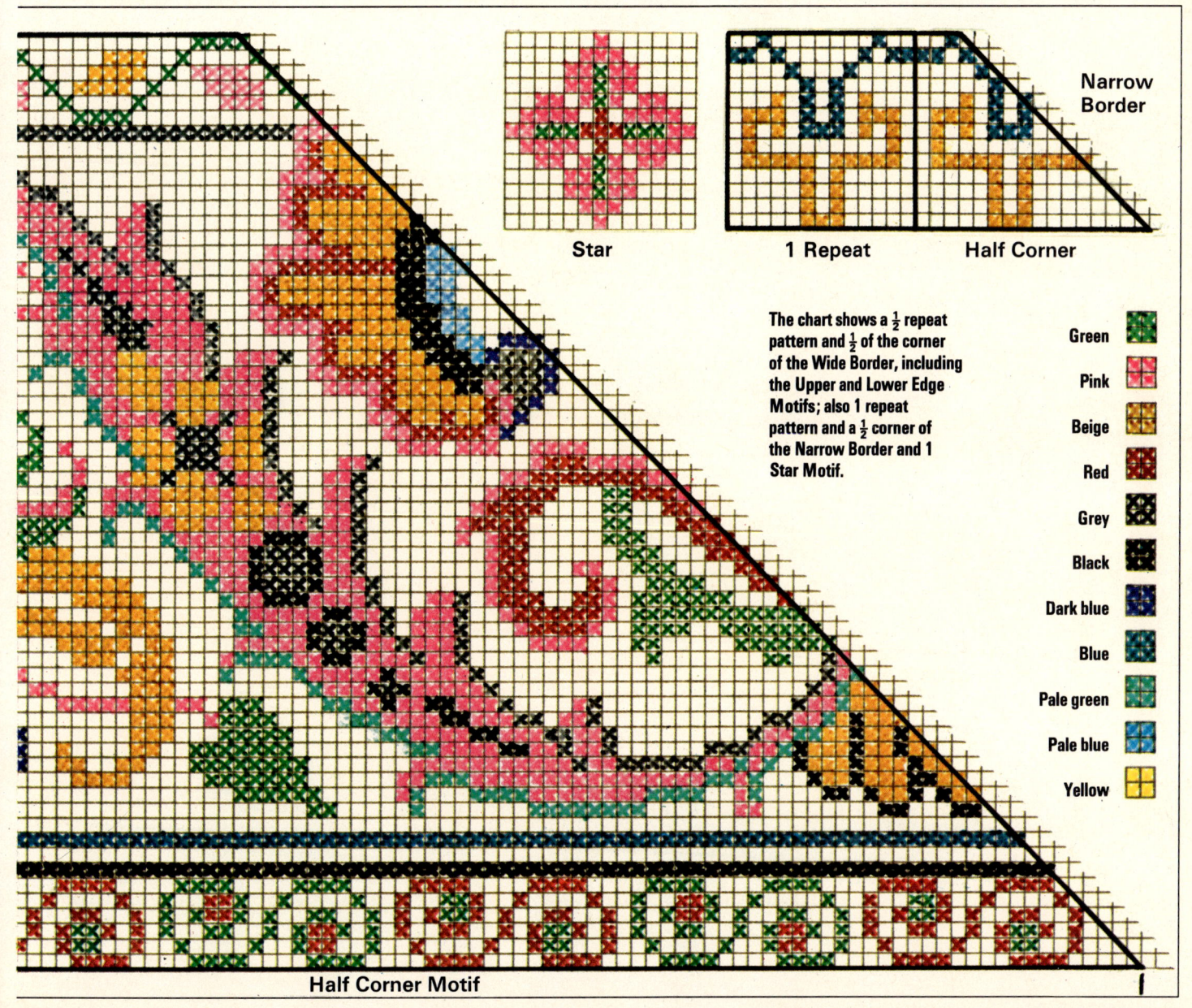

Star

1 Repeat **Half Corner**

Narrow Border

The chart shows a ½ repeat pattern and ½ of the corner of the Wide Border, including the Upper and Lower Edge Motifs; also 1 repeat pattern and a ½ corner of the Narrow Border and 1 Star Motif.

Green
Pink
Beige
Red
Grey
Black
Dark blue
Blue
Pale green
Pale blue
Yellow

Half Corner Motif

The pattern for this embroidered silk dress is given in sizes C and E on Pattern Sheet 75, Style 3. Directions are for size C. Changes for size E are in square brackets.

Smooth as silk

The repeat pattern for the embroidery motif is shown here actual size.

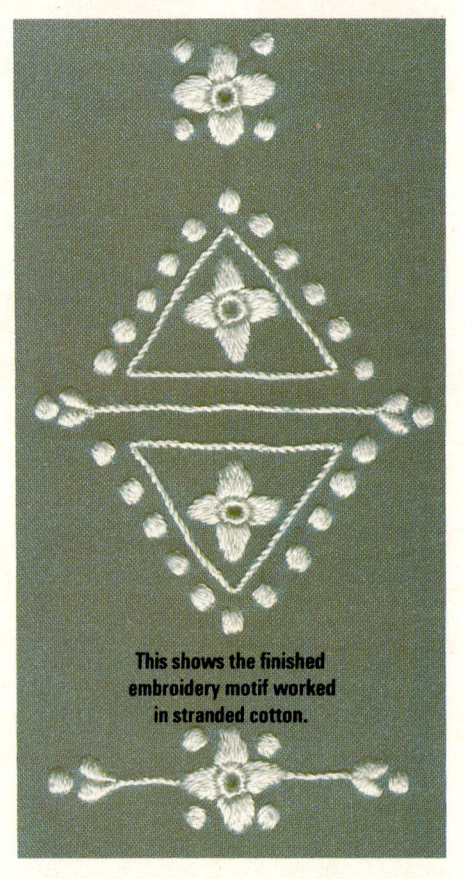

This shows the finished embroidery motif worked in stranded cotton.

Materials Required: Silk: 4.50 [4.60] m (4$\frac{7}{8}$ yds [5 yds]), 90 cm (36") wide. Fine white linen: 0.35 m ($\frac{3}{8}$ yd), 90 cm (36") wide. 5 buttons. Stranded embroidery cotton: 1 skein grey.

Cutting out: See cutting layout. Add 1.5 cm ($\frac{5}{8}$") seam allowances and 4 cm (1$\frac{1}{2}$") for hem. Cut 2 bias strips to bind the sleeve slits, each 4 cm (1$\frac{1}{2}$") wide and 14 cm (5$\frac{1}{2}$") long. From linen, cut out 1 stand-up collar, front facings to end of opening, and cuffs up to the fold line.

Before embroidering: Finish cut edges of fronts. Trace motif and transfer onto the bodice with dressmaker's carbon paper. On both fronts, place the motif 11[12] cm (4$\frac{3}{8}$"[4$\frac{3}{4}$"]) from yoke seam and 6.5[7] cm (2$\frac{5}{8}$"[2$\frac{3}{4}$"]) from front edge, measured from upper and side edge of motif. Repeat the diamond pattern and the single flower once more below the first motif.

Embroidering: Work all lines in stem stitch and all solid areas in satin stitch with 2 strands of embroidery thread. Embroider the ring at the flower center in close satin stitch or buttonhole stitch, then cut out the fabric center with very sharp scissors.

Sewing: Sewing instructions are given under Style 3 on Pattern Sheet 75. All top-stitched lines are worked in grey.

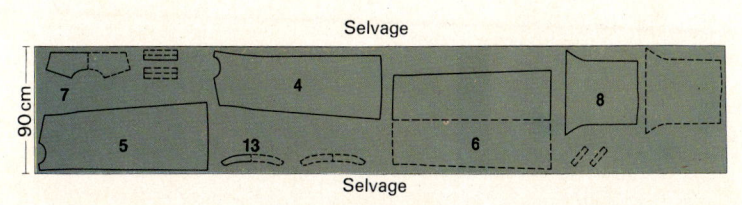

◀ Cutting layout for 90 cm (36") wide fabric. Cut out in single fabric.

2399

In keeping with tradition

A traditional pattern in blue on white always makes an inviting table setting. We've matched the motif on the cloth to the design on the china — a clever idea for you to try sometime with your own tableware or plain white or blue china.

The tablecloth illustrated is square with the main motif in the centre and a border all around the edge.

Size of cloth: 150 cm (59") square.

Materials Required:
White linen: 160 cm (63") square. Stranded cotton: 17 skeins blue.

Making the cloth
Turn a 5 cm (2") hem to the right side, mitering the corners. Turn in the raw edge and stitch the hem close to the edge.

Mark the center of the cloth horizontally and vertically with basting. Trace the central motif ($\frac{1}{2}$ is given on the pattern) and transfer to the cloth with dressmaker's carbon paper. Distribute the 8 small motifs evenly around the central motif as shown in the small photograph on the far right.
Place the border motifs so that the outer edge of the motifs is 16 cm ($6\frac{1}{4}$") from the edge of the cloth, making sure that they are equidistant. Place a corner motif at each corner as shown right.

Working the embroidery
With undivided strands, the lines are worked in stem stitch, the large dots in satin stitch, the small dots with French knots.

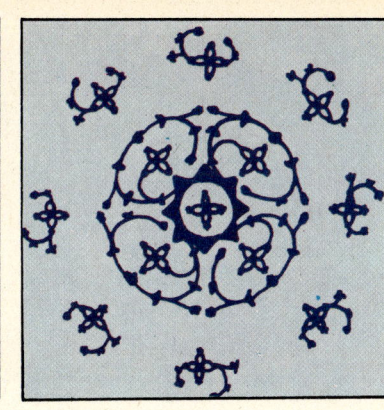

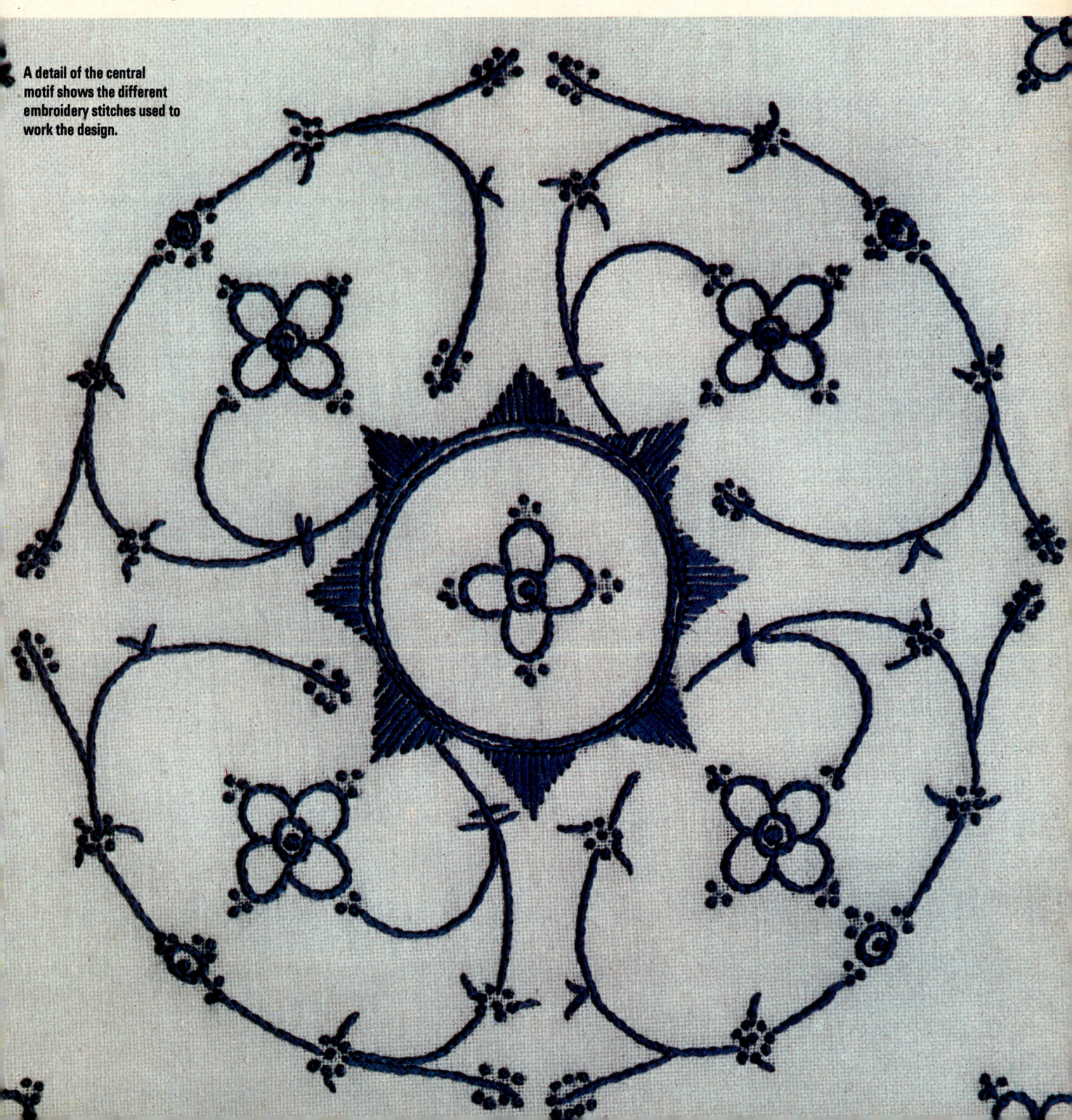

A detail of the central motif shows the different embroidery stitches used to work the design.

Design for a tablecloth

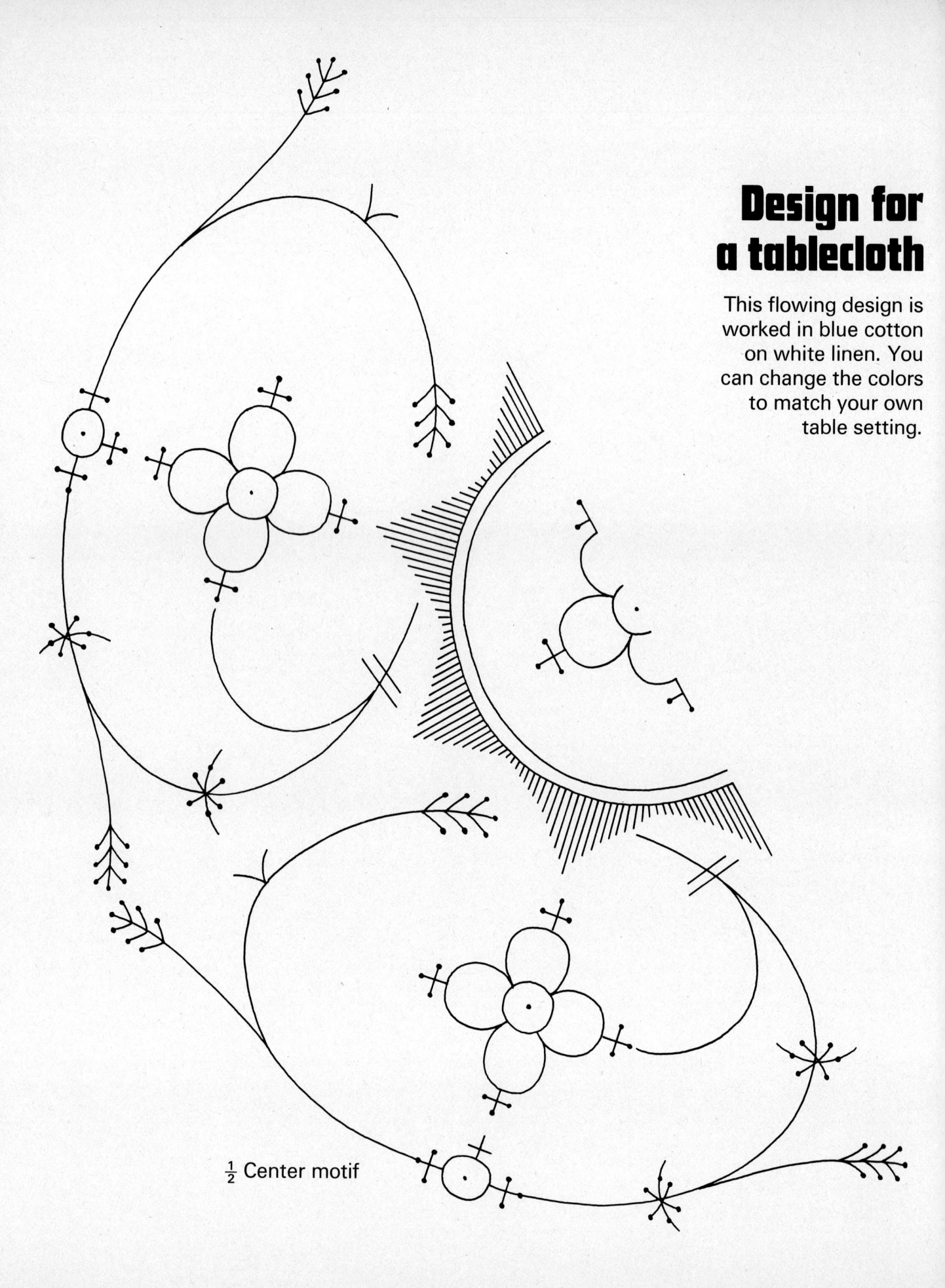

This flowing design is worked in blue cotton on white linen. You can change the colors to match your own table setting.

½ Center motif

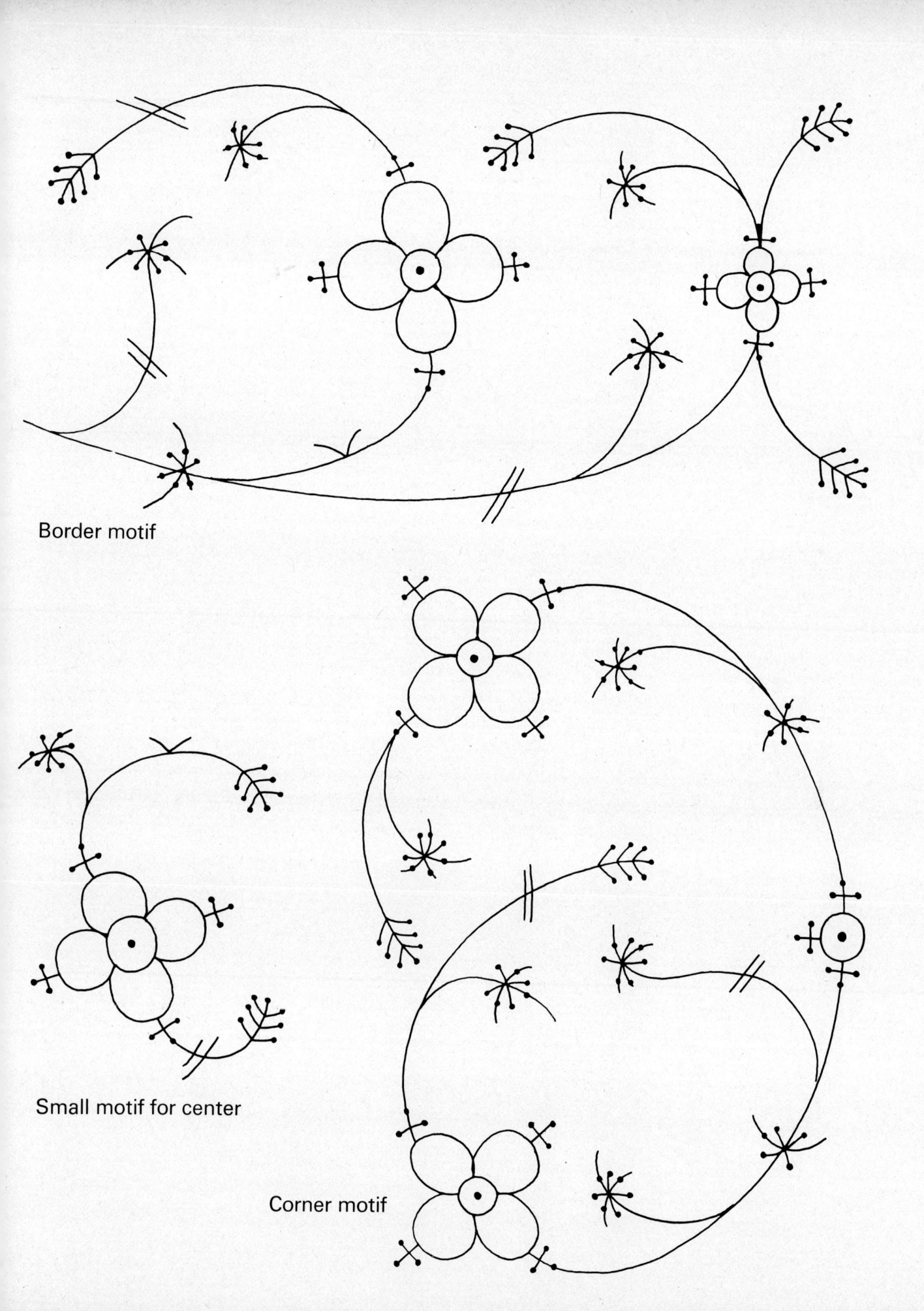

Border motif

Small motif for center

Corner motif

A fresh-looking breakfast tablecloth with a crochet border. Alternate squares are embroidered with flowers and are then joined with a blanket stitch insertion.

A bright tablecloth for a cheery breakfast

Summer flowers for a table

Embroidery

Crochet

Size: 130 cm (51") square, including crocheted edging.

Materials Required:
Stranded cotton: 3 skeins white, 10 skeins red. Crochet cotton for joining the squares and working the edging: 150 gm or 6 oz blue. Crochet hook size D. Blue-and-white gingham fabric: 2.8 m, 85 cm wide (3¼ yds, 36" wide).

Cutting out the squares
Cut 36 pieces of blue-and-white gingham fabric, each measuring approximately 22.2 cm (8¾") square. Turn under a 1.3 cm (½") hem all round the edge of each

◀ The separate squares of fabric are joined with a blanket stitch insertion. The threads linking the squares must not be pulled too tightly so that they space between the pieces of fabric.

square, mitering the corners. Slip-stitch the hem.

Embroidering the squares
Trace the 18 flower motifs and transfer a different one onto 18 squares of fabric with dressmaker's carbon paper, positioning them in the center. Stretch the fabric on an embroidery frame or in a hoop. Embroider the flowers in straight, slanting, or long and short satin stitch, using all 6 strands of red stranded cotton. Work the flower centers in white satin stitch, the dots in French knots, and the dividing lines in stem stitch.

Joining the squares
When the embroidery is complete, press all 36 squares from the wrong

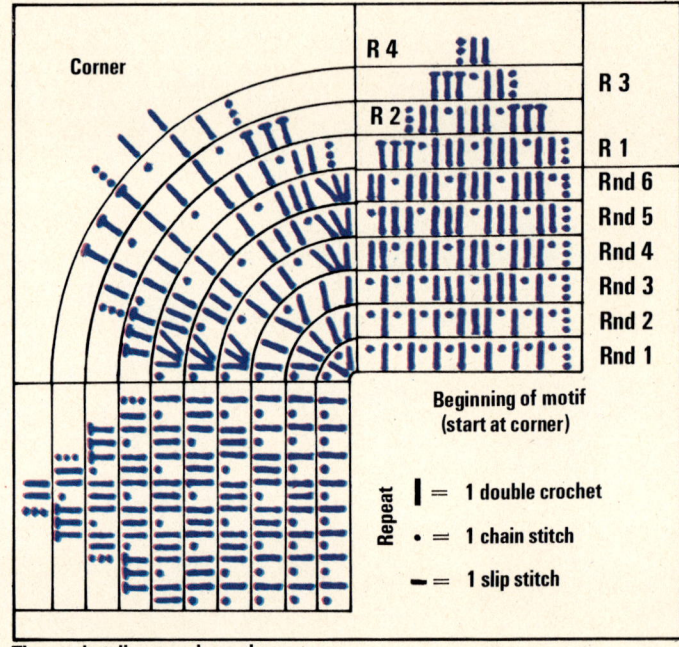

The crochet diagram above shows how to begin the rounds, how to work a corner and how to work the repeat pattern which is continued all along the sides. The detail photograph (left) shows the same section of the border.

side and join them, alternating the embroidered and plain ones. First place 2 squares one above the other and work the horizontal seam with blanket stitch insertion. Work 4 blanket stitches into the first check of the upper square, then 4 blanket stitches into the second check of the lower square. Continue in this way into every 2nd check of alternate squares. Leave the thread fairly loose so that an openwork effect is achieved.

Make 6 strips of 6 squares each by joining them in the same way. Then join the 6 strips together lengthwise, again using blanket stitch insertion. Finally, finish off the outer edge of the cloth with groups of 4 blanket stitches into alternate checks and 5 blanket stitches into each corner.

Crocheting the edging
The edging is worked in rounds from the right side of the cloth.
Abbreviations: St(s) = stitch(es). Dc = double crochet. R = row(s). Rnd(s) = round(s).
Rnd 1: Fasten the yarn into the last blanket st at one of the corners. Make 4 ch, *1 dc into the 1st blanket st, 1 ch, 1 dc into the 4th blanket st, 1 ch, repeat from * to end, always inserting the hook into the blanket stitch from front to back as shown in the photograph at the right. Finish this and all following rnds with 1 slip st into the 3rd ch of the 4 ch at the beginning of the rnd.
Rnds 2–6 of the border and Rnds 1–4 of the points: Follow the crochet diagram given at the left.

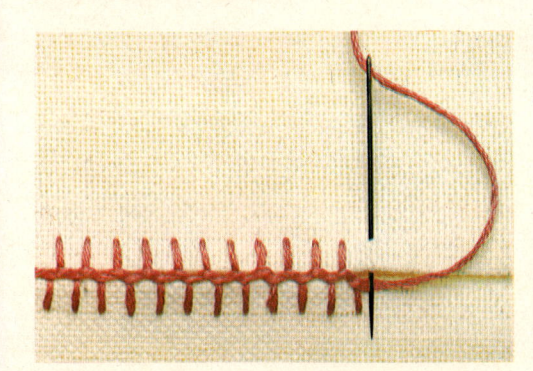

Blanket stitch insertion

How-to

Single blanket stitch

1 Insert the needle through the double fabric, about 0.5 cm ($\frac{3}{16}$") from the outer edge. The thread should lie under the needle point.

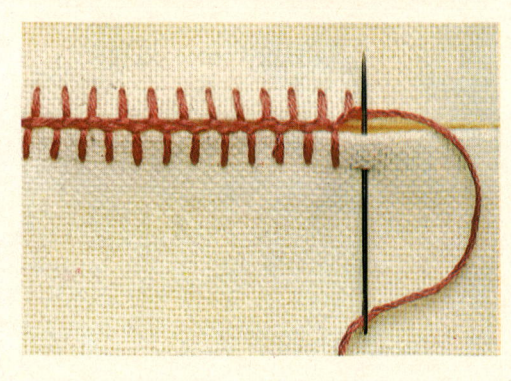

2 On the lower fabric, work the stitches the other way up. Alternate the lower stitches with those on the upper piece.

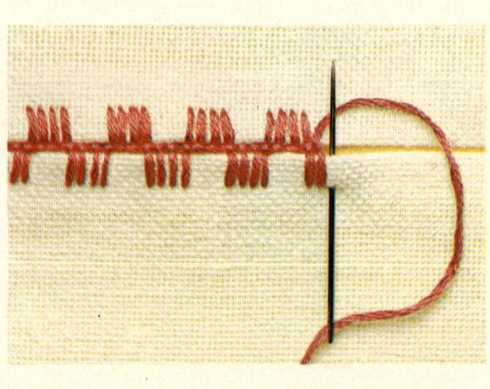

Blanket stitch in groups

3 For a bolder pattern, work 4 blanket stitches close together to form a little block. Alternate blocks between the upper and lower fabric pieces.

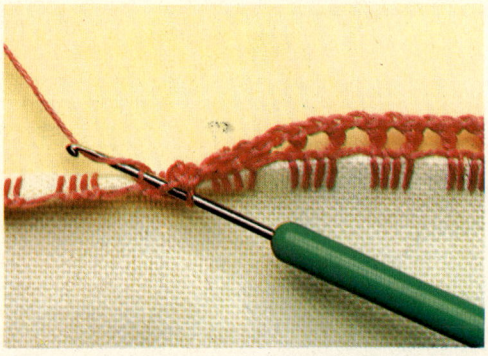

4 To crochet the edging, work the double crochets into the first and fourth blanket stitches. Insert the hook into the stitches from front to back.

Pick your flower

Work some pretty flowers onto a tablecloth with simple embroidery stitches. There's a whole bouquet from which to choose!

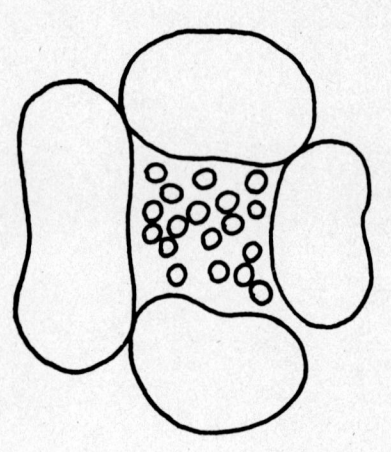

2409

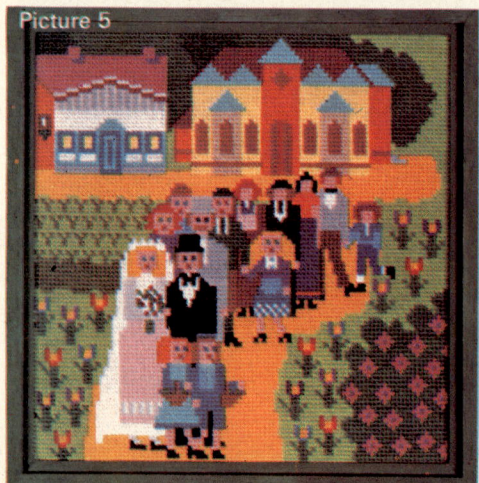

Picture 5

Picture 3

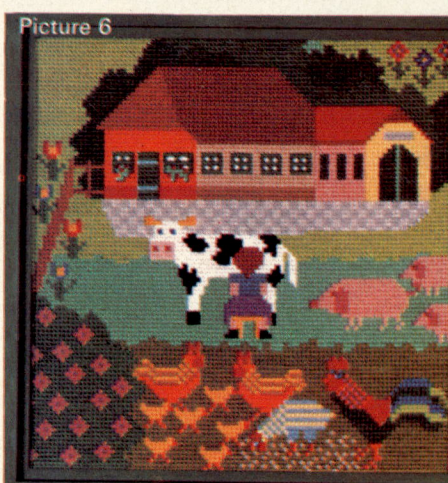

Picture 6

2410

A day in the country

If you enjoy canvaswork on a grand scale, this cross-stitch picture is for you. The design has been divided into 6 separate sections, so if the large picture is too daunting, you can make one or two of the smaller pictures.

Sizes: Approximately 75cm x 50cm (30" x 20") or 25cm (10") square.

Materials Required: Double-thread canvas, 20 holes to 5cm (10 holes to 1"), 70cm (27") wide: For the large picture, 0.95m (1yd), for every 2 small ones, 0.35m ($\frac{3}{8}$yd). Stranded embroidery cotton: quantities for the large picture are shown overleaf, while quantities for the smaller ones are given below.

Picture 1: 1 skein each of colors 1, 2, 3, 4, 5, 6, 7, 8, 10, 11, 15, 19, 20, 21, 22, 23, 24, 25, 27, 28, 29, 30; 2 skeins each of colors 14 and 18; 3 skeins of color 17.

Picture 2: 1 skein each of colors 1, 2, 4, 5, 6, 8, 9, 10, 11, 15, 19, 20, 21, 22, 23, 24, 25, 26, 27, 28, 29, 30; 2 skeins each of colors 3, 14, 18; 3 skeins of color 17.

Picture 3: 1 skein each of colors 1, 2, 3, 4, 5, 6, 7, 8, 9, 10, 11, 12, 15, 16, 19, 20, 21, 22, 23, 24, 25, 26, 27, 29, 30; 2 skeins each of colors 14 and 18; 3 skeins of color 17.

Picture 4: 1 skein each of colors 1, 2, 3, 4, 5, 6, 7, 8, 9, 10, 11, 12, 15, 16, 18, 19, 21, 22, 23, 25, 26, 27, 28, 29, 30; 2 skeins of color 20; 3 skeins of color 17.

Picture 5: 1 skein each of colors 1, 2, 4, 5, 6, 7, 8, 9, 10, 11, 12, 13, 14, 15, 16, 19, 21, 22, 23, 26, 27, 28, 29, 30; 2 skeins each of colors 3 and 20; 3 skeins of color 17.

Picture 6: 1 skein each of color 1, 2, 3, 4, 5, 6, 7, 8, 9, 10, 11, 14, 15, 16, 18, 21, 22, 23, 24, 26, 27, 28, 29, 30; 2 skeins each of colors 17 and 20.

Making the pictures

Chart for large picture is shown overleaf. Heavy lines divide it into the 6 smaller pictures shown here. (They are arranged out of order so that you can see how each looks separately.) Each square on the chart represents 1 cross-stitch. Mark center of canvas both ways. On the large picture, leave a border of about 10cm (4") all around. On the smaller pictures, leave a 5cm (2") border all around. Mount on canvaswork frame if desired. Begin in the center, and with undivided strands, work in cross-stitch over 1 pair of canvas threads in height and width. Block canvas if necessary when design is complete. Stretch work over piece of hardboard and frame as desired.

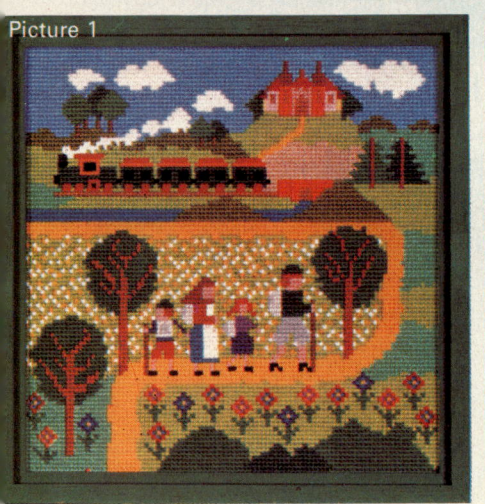

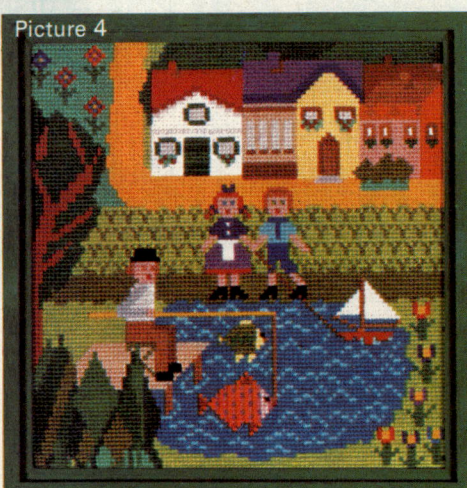

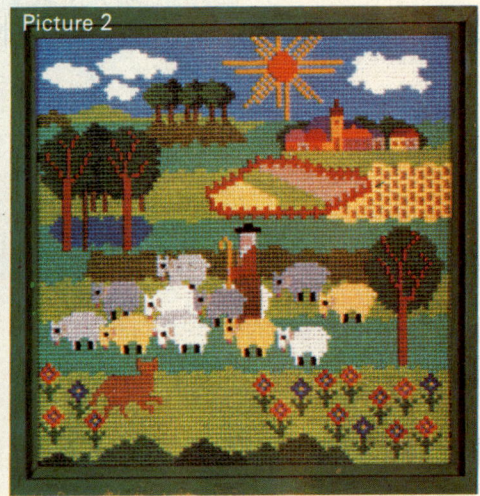

2412

1 white	5 skeins
2 yellow	3 skeins
3 gold	7 skeins
4 orange	4 skeins
5 scarlet	3 skeins
6 maroon	2 skeins
7 pale pink	2 skeins
8 flesh	2 skeins
9 pink	4 skeins
10 mauve	3 skeins
11 purple	2 skeins
12 navy	2 skeins
13 blue-grey	1 skein
14 sky blue	7 skeins
15 mid blue	6 skeins
16 turquoise	3 skeins
17 lime green	17 skeins
18 grass green	8 skeins
19 leaf green	3 skeins
20 dark green	9 skeins
21 bottle green	4 skeins
22 olive green	5 skeins
23 beige	3 skeins
24 mid brown	1 skein
25 pale tan	3 skeins
26 tan	3 skeins
27 chestnut	2 skeins
28 pale grey	3 skeins
29 dark grey	2 skeins
30 black	2 skeins

Chart for the large picture: Each colored square represents one cross-stitch. Colors and quantities for the whole picture are given above.

2413

Seating arrangements

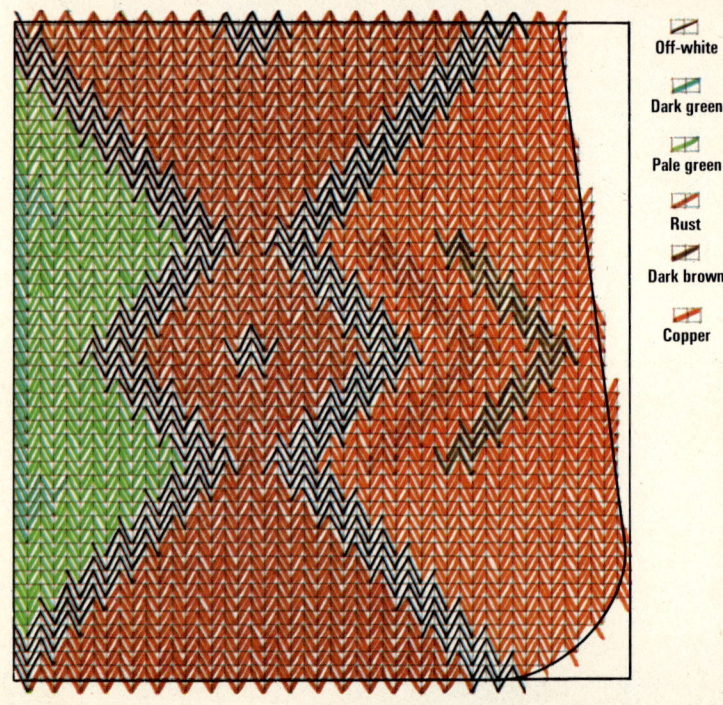

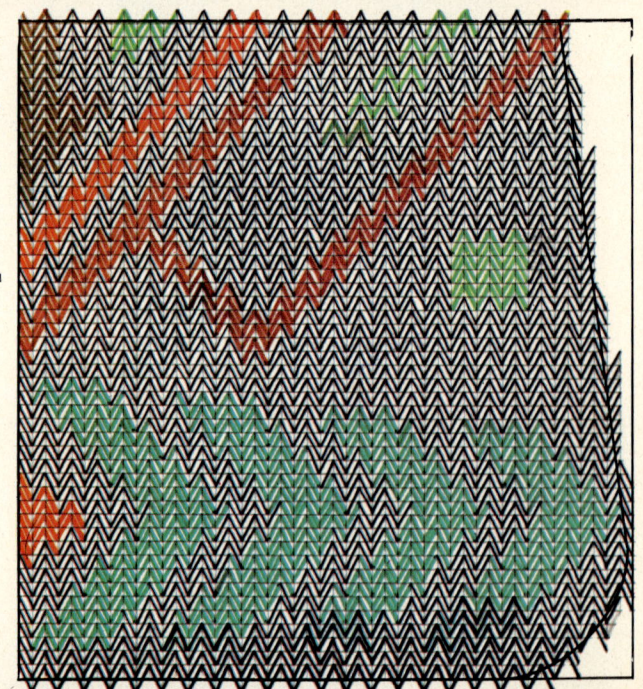

Off-white
Dark green
Pale green
Rust
Dark brown
Copper

Add comfort and style to a plain wooden chair with a canvaswork cushion. The designs on the cushions illustrated are worked in Kalem (or knitted) stitch for an unusual effect.

*

Size: About 40 x 40 cm (15¾" x 15¾").

Materials Required:
Skeined rug wool in 25 gm (1 oz) skeins: <u>Cushion 1:</u> 2 skeins rust; 1 skein each off-white, copper, dark green, pale green, and dark brown. <u>Cushion 2:</u> 4 skeins off-white, 1 skein each dark green, pale green, copper, rust, and dark brown. <u>For 2 cushions:</u> Binca or canvas: 45 cm (½ yd), 107 cm (42") wide, 24 squares to 10 cm (4"). Batting or wadding: 80 cm x 80 cm (31½" x 31½"). Backing fabric: 45 cm (½ yd), 90 cm (36") wide. Twisted cord in a matching color: 5 m (5½ yds).

Working the embroidery
A quarter of each design is given on the color chart. Outline all the shapes first in the relevant colors, then fill in the background and the center of the shapes in up and down rows. Work 2 further rows on all sides beyond the actual size of the cushion in order to avoid the base fabric showing through when sewing together.

Making the cushion
Trim the excess fabric to about 1 cm (⅜") all around. Stitch to the backing and turn, leaving a 20 cm (8") opening in one side. Now pad the cushions with 2 layers of batting or wadding and sew up. Cut the twisted cord to the circumference of the cushion and sew it around the edge. For the tapes (to tie to the chair), stitch on 2 cords about 40 cm (16") long in an appropriate position.

Kalem or knitted stitch

How-to

Each complete V-shaped Kalem stitch is worked over 2 squares upward and across. It is worked one row at a time, whether you work horizontally, vertically, or diagonally.

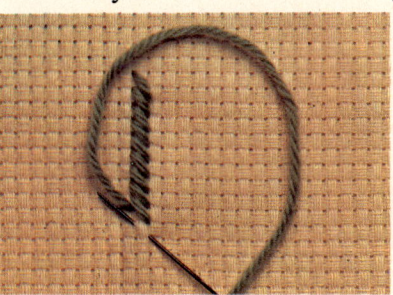

Work 1st row from top to bottom. Insert the needle 2 squares down and 1 across. Bring out 1 diagonal square up, ready for next stitch.

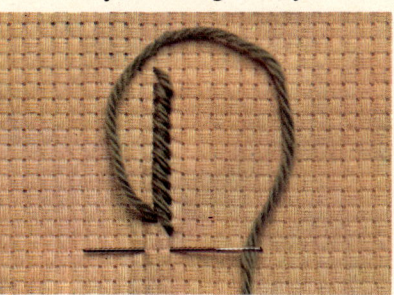

The connecting stitch of one vertical row to the next is always made horizontally by passing the needle across behind 2 squares.

In 2nd row, work from bottom to top. Insert needle 2 squares up and 1 across (into same hole as top of stitch in previous row). Emerge 1 diagonal square down.

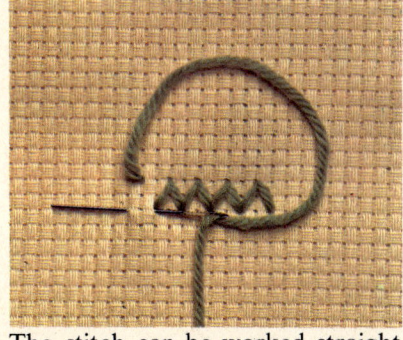

The stitch can be worked straight across for horizontal outlines. Work each complete stitch over 2 squares in height and width. Begin next row 1 square down.

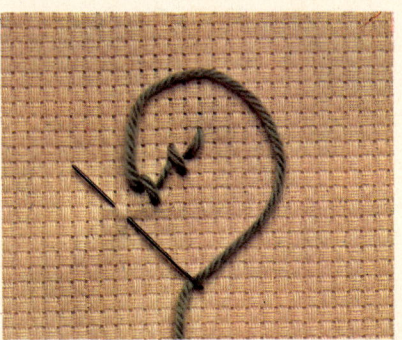

This stitch can also be worked diagonally as an outline stitch for the diagonal areas of the design. Embroider alternately sloping stitches top right to bottom left.

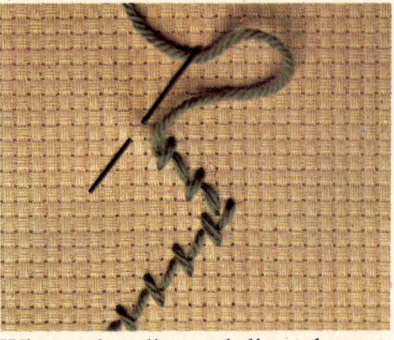

Where the diagonal line changes direction to form a point, the work must be turned. Work a row of alternately sloping stitches from bottom right to top left.

2415

It's a relief

This design is an unusual variation on a latch hook rug. It is worked with pre-cut rug yarn in two lengths to form a stunning relief pattern.

Size: Approximately 160 cm x 107 cm (63" x 42").
Materials Required: Rug canvas with 13 holes to 10 cm (10 holes to 3"): 1.75 m (1$\frac{7}{8}$ yds), 122 cm (48") wide. Rya yarn in pre-cut packs of 500 pieces: 106 packs light amber. Rug yarn in pre-cut packs of 320 pieces: 32 packs dark amber; 5 packs light amber. Latch hook. Carpet tape: 5.50 m (6 yds).

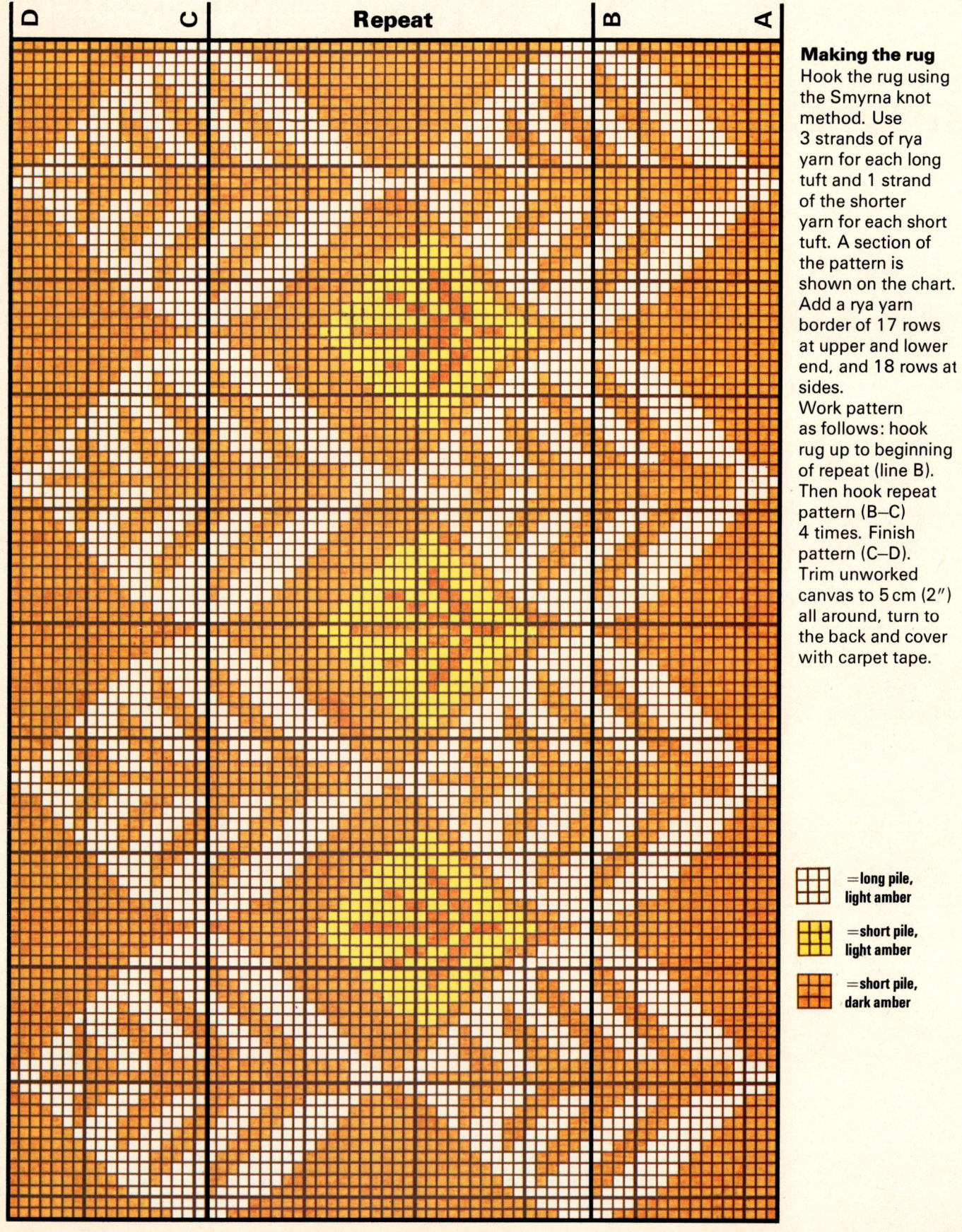

Making the rug

Hook the rug using the Smyrna knot method. Use 3 strands of rya yarn for each long tuft and 1 strand of the shorter yarn for each short tuft. A section of the pattern is shown on the chart. Add a rya yarn border of 17 rows at upper and lower end, and 18 rows at sides.

Work pattern as follows: hook rug up to beginning of repeat (line B). Then hook repeat pattern (B–C) 4 times. Finish pattern (C–D). Trim unworked canvas to 5 cm (2") all around, turn to the back and cover with carpet tape.

= long pile, light amber

= short pile, light amber

= short pile, dark amber

There are twelve different patterns in this patchwork rug, so you will never get bored while you are hooking! By limiting the colors to a particular range such as tones of yellow and green, you can ensure that the effect is not fussy.

Making the rug
Size: Each single square measures 30 cm x 30 cm (11¾" x 11¾") and the whole rug measures 1.20 m x 1.80 m (47½" x 71").

The squares can be worked individually or in sections of squares which are pieced together. In this way, the rug can be enlarged or reduced to the size required to fit your floor. Our rug is made in two sections of twelve squares each and we show you two methods of joining canvas — a necessary process when the canvas is not as wide as the whole rug.

The 12 patterns incorporate 9 different colors (Materials Required and Color Key are given overleaf). They are worked from the Rug Chart, overleaf, with the Ghiordes knot technique, using pre-cut rug yarn and a latch hook. When the sections have been knotted and pieced together, the outer edges of the rug are overcast with skeined rug yarn.

Important: Before beginning to knot, plan exactly how you wish to arrange the squares, as all pieces must be knotted in the same direction.

Making the cushions
Size: 40 cm (15¾") square. The Materials Required, Color Key, and Chart are given overleaf. Follow the design from the Rug Chart, extending the pattern until the piece is the required dimension. The edges are overcast with skeined rug wool as for the rug. For the backing, cut a square of fabric in a matching color, stitch around 3 sides and then insert a zipper into the 4th side. Stuff with a cushion pad slightly larger all around than the cover.

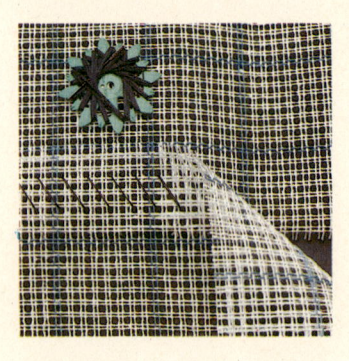

The Ghiordes Knot: Insert the hook under the lower of the double threads. Catch in a strand of yarn and draw through about two-thirds of it down to the right. Place the short end over to the left. Insert the hook under the upper thread and place the long end over the latch. Draw the hook down, pull the yarn through and a knot is formed.

Method 1 for joining canvas: The canvas can be pieced together before knotting. Overlap the pieces as shown above, matching the upper and lower layers of threads exactly. Baste the pieces together with large stitches, using strong carpet thread, then knot the rug yarn through both layers of canvas at once (the ordinary Smyrna knot is shown in the photograph). The pile will hide the join completely.

Method 2 for joining canvas: Work the separate sections, leaving a few rows of excess canvas at the edges. Then place the sections together, right sides facing, matching up the patterns and making sure the knots lie in the same direction. Pin together with large pins and sew along the edge with backstitch. Open out the excess canvas flat along the seams and baste loosely to the back to hold it down. If it is a cut edge, it should be overcast first to prevent fraying.

2418

Squares for a patchwork rug

Get hooked

Complement the rug with a few cushions in matching patterns.

Materials Required: For the 2 rug sections of 12 squares each: Rug canvas with 13 holes to 10 cm (10 holes to 3″): 2.70 m (3 yds), 90 cm (36″) wide (to be worked as 2 sections). Latch hook. Pre-cut rug yarn (see Color Key):

Color 1   11 packs
Color 2   11 packs
Color 3   13 packs
Color 4   18 packs
Color 5   13 packs
Color 6   13 packs
Color 7   18 packs
Color 8   10 packs
Color 9   8 packs

Skeined yarn: 200 gm (8 oz). Color 6.

Materials for Cushion 1:
Color 8   3 packs
Color 4   4 packs
Color 7   2 packs
Color 2   2 packs
Skeined yarn: 50 gm (2 oz) Color 4. Rug canvas: 40 cm x 45 cm (15¾″ x 17¾″).

Materials for Cushion 2:
Color 4   2 packs
Color 6   2 packs
Color 5   2 packs
Color 9   1 pack
Color 2   2 packs
Color 8   1 pack
Color 7   1 pack
Skeined yarn: 50 gm (2 oz) Color 6. Rug canvas: 40 cm x 45 cm (15¾″ x 17¾″).

Materials for Cushion 3:
Color 5   3 packs
Color 8   3 packs
Color 7   3 packs
Skeined yarn: 50 gm (2 oz) Color 5. Rug canvas: 40 cm x 45 cm (15¾″ x 17¾″).

The chart shows the 12 patterns for the rug squares. They are each 39 knots square or 30 cm x 30 cm (11¾″ x 11¾″). The Color Key at the side indicates the color used in each case. The colors used for the chart are slightly different from the actual colors for easier identification.

2420

Color 1
Color 2
Color 3
Color 4
Color 5
Color 6
Color 7
Color 8
Color 9

2421

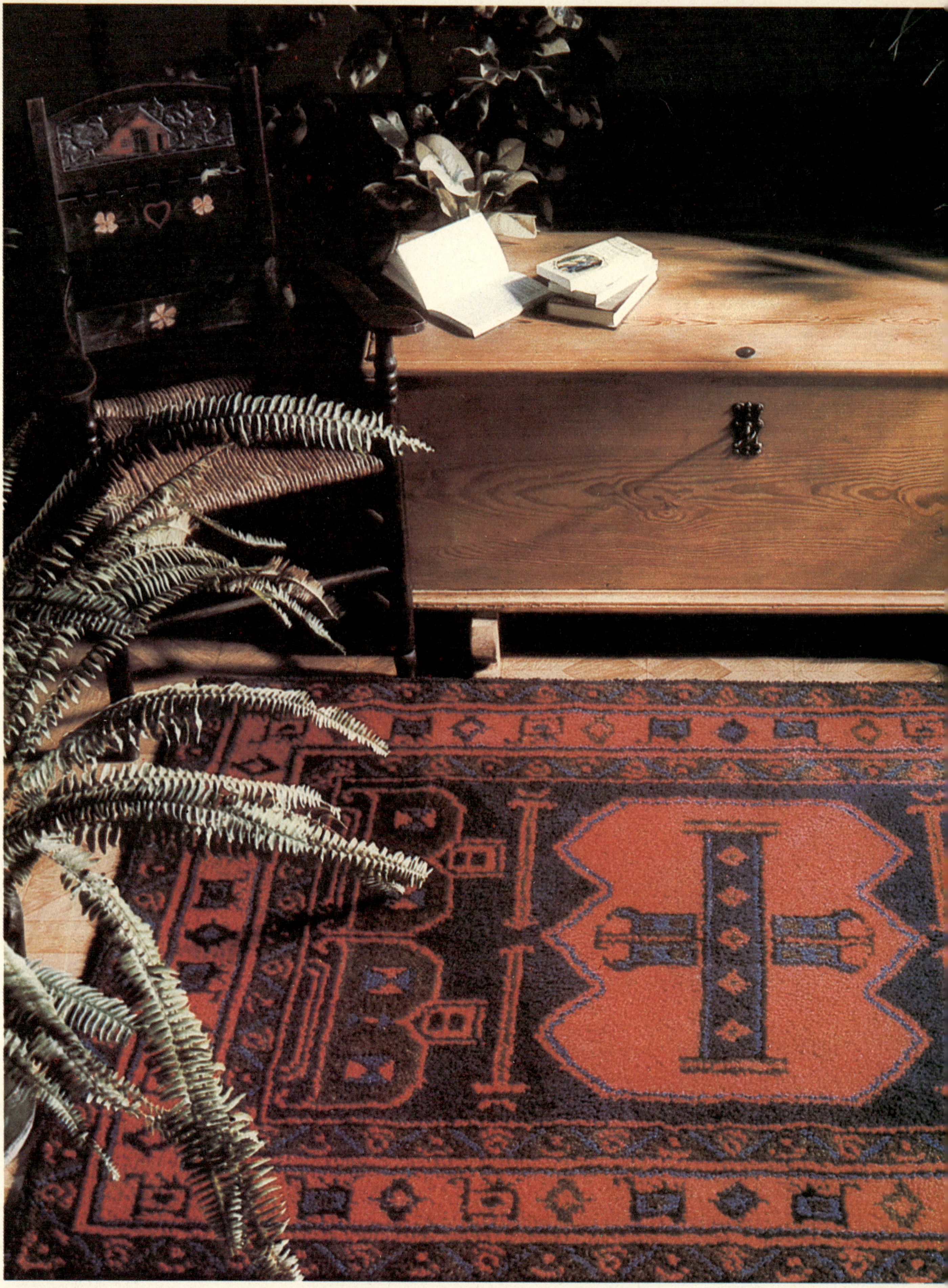

Crafts

From a Caucasian design

In glowing hues

A sumptuous eastern rug is a fashionable and valuable addition to the home. Make this one in five dark, rich colors, following a pattern adapted from an original Caucasian design. The Ghiordes knot technique is used with pre-cut rug wool.

Materials Required:
Rug canvas, 10 holes to 7.5 cm (3"): 4.40 m (4$\frac{7}{8}$ yds), 90 cm (36") wide. Rug wool in pre-cut packs of 320 strands in the following colors and quantities: 59 packs red, 38 packs dark blue, 31 packs medium brown, 16 packs each of blue and dark brown. Latch hook. Carpet binding tape. Heavy duty thread.

Size: The rug illustrated measures 150 cm x 200 cm (59" x 78$\frac{3}{4}$"). To obtain the full width, it is worked on two strips of canvas which are joined before commencing the knotting. First, cut the length of canvas in half, then cut off one of the selvages on each of the new lengths. Overlap these edges by 2.5 cm – 3.8 cm (1" – 1$\frac{1}{2}$"), matching holes and threads precisely. Stitch the pieces together securely along each raw edge, using strong thread. The rug can now be hooked through both layers of canvas to make a firm join.

Making the rug
Work the design with the Ghiordes knot by following the chart, overleaf. Each square represents one knot. Leaving a border of about 7.5 cm (3") all round, begin knotting with the full length of the rug stretching away from you on a large table or workbench. Start in the lower left-hand corner of the canvas and work in parallel rows across the canvas from left to right or vice-versa if left-handed. Never work small areas of color at random because the pile will not blend together and this will give a very patchy appearance to the finished rug.

BEGIN HERE ▶

Following the chart

The chart for the rug illustrated is shown opposite. A color key is also given. Each square on the chart represents one knot on the canvas. Turn the chart so that the arrow corresponds with the lower left-hand corner of the canvas. A quarter of the design is shown; work the other three quarters as you come to them by reversing the pattern.

Instead of counting out the squares on the chart as you work, you may prefer to paint the design onto the canvas before beginning to knot. Use a hard paint brush and acrylic paint, placing the canvas on sheets of newspaper on a table or on the floor before you begin. Paint each square of canvas to correspond to each square on the chart. Leave to dry thoroughly before knotting. You can now simply match the wool to the appropriate colors on the canvas, without constantly referring to the chart.

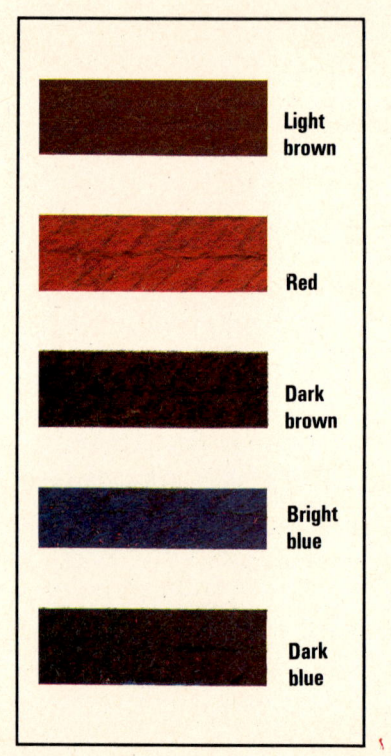

	Light brown
	Red
	Dark brown
	Bright blue
	Dark blue

2424

2425

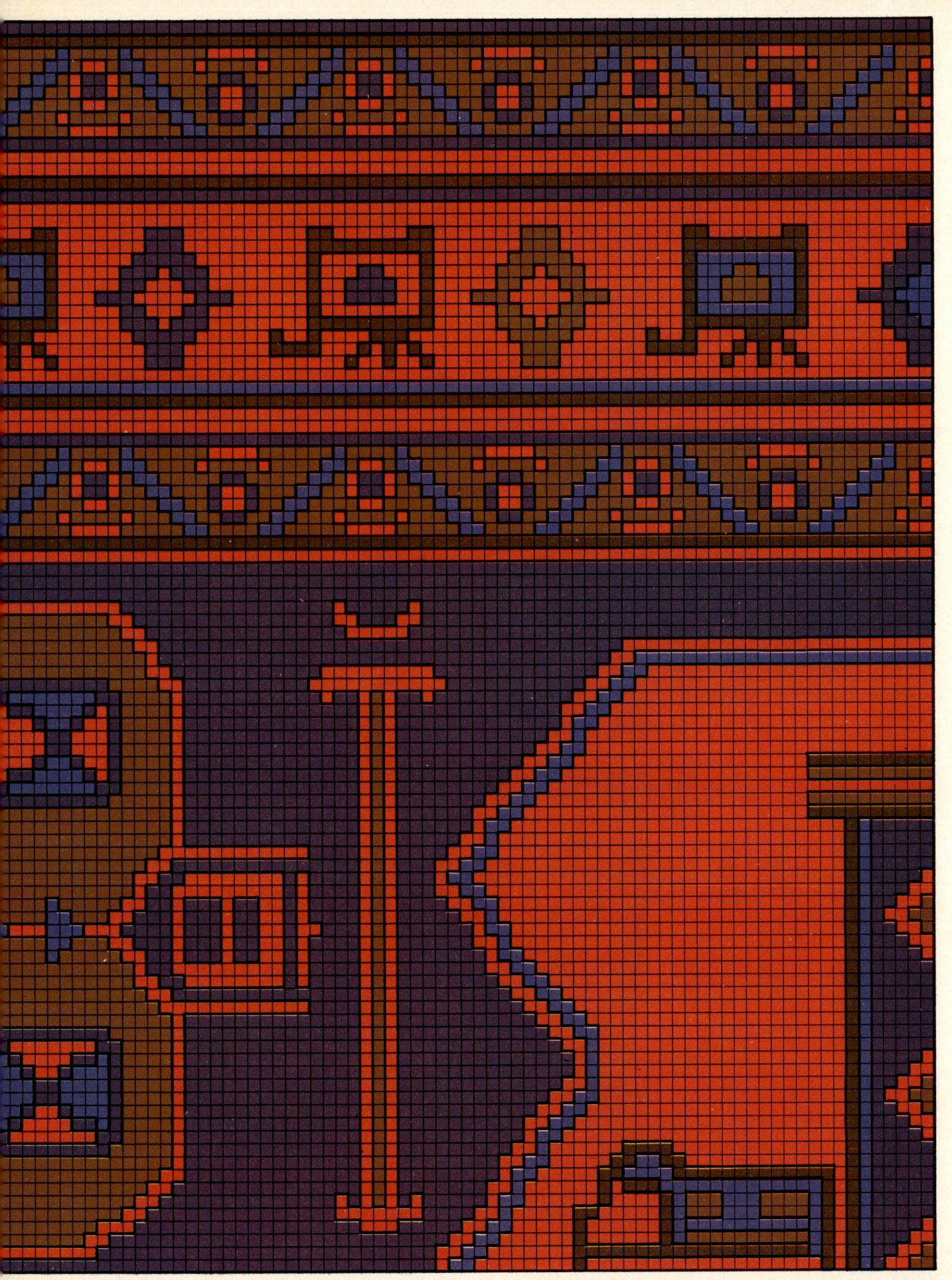

How-to

Knotting the rug

The Ghiordes knot

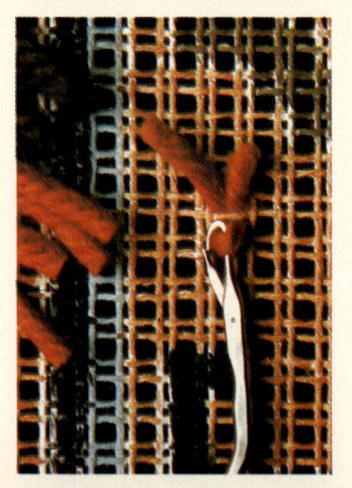

1 Insert the hook and latch under the lower of the double threads. Place the yarn into the hook and, holding the left-hand end, pull just over half the right-hand end through.

2 Now insert the hook and latch under the upper of the double threads. Place right-hand end of yarn across the hook from right to left and pull the hook down so that a knot is made.

3 The knots are worked in rows from left to right. Change color according to the chart and make sure that the yarn ends are as even as possible.

Painting the canvas

1 Paint the design onto the canvas, square by square, following the colors on the chart. Then knot the yarn to match the colors on the canvas.

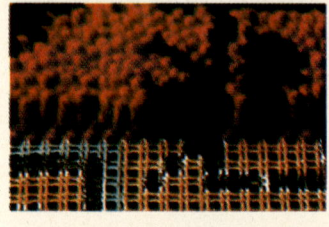

2 Here, the painted canvas has been partially knotted. The pile on the rug is about 2.5 cm (1″) high.

3 Finish the raw edge of the rug by trimming the canvas to about 4 cm (1½″), folding it under, mitering the corners and either basting or gluing it down. Then sew or glue wide carpet binding tape against the folded edge. Miter the corners of the tape and then secure the other edge.

Index

Appliqué
  pillow 2386
  tablecloth 2388
Aran pullover, knitted
  man's 2317
  woman's 2315, 2318
Bag, bicycle 2376
Beads, crocheting with 2350
Bedspread, crocheted 2339, 2342, 2344
Bicycle bag, sewn 2376
Blanket stitch, embroidered 2407
Blazer, woman's sewn 2372
Blouse, woman's
  embroidered 2390
  sewn 2390
Body measurements chart 2313
Bolero, woman's crocheted 2351
Button fastening on a pleat 2371
Buttonhole, hand-sewn 2374
Canvaswork
  cushion 2414
  Kalem stitch 2415
  knitted stitch 2415
  picture 2410
Cardigan, crocheted
  man's 2358
  woman's 2353
Centimeter
  conversion to inches 2312
  ruler 2313
Chair, cushion for 2414
Children
  bag, bicycle 2376
  costume, Indian 2378
  dress, sewn 2360
  shirt, sewn 2360
  toy hand puppets, sewn 2380
Costume, child's sewn 2378
Crafts
  canvaswork
    cushion 2414
    picture 2410
  rugmaking
    hooked 2416, 2418, 2422
    sewn patchwork 2382
Crochet
  beads, with 2350
  bedspread 2339, 2342, 2344

  bolero, woman's 2351
  cardigan
    man's 2358
    woman's 2353
  double crochet
    clusters 2346
    diamonds in relief 2358
  hat, woman's 2356
  jacket
    man's 2358
    woman's 2356
  mat 2338
  pillow 2339
  relief double crochet, diamonds in 2358
  ruffles 2341
  star stitch 2355
  stitch
    double crochet
      clusters 2346
      diamond in relief 2358
    star 2355
    strawberry 2352
  strawberry pattern 2352
  tablecloth border 2404
  vest, woman's 2347, 2349
Cross-stitch
  canvaswork picture 2410
  on knitting 2324
  tablecloth 2396
Cushion—see also Pillow
Cushion, chair 2414
Dress
  child's, sewn 2360
  woman's
    embroidered 2398
    sewn 2368, 2398
Dressmaking—see Sewing
Embroidery
  blanket stitch
    group 2407
    insertion 2407
    single 2407
  blouse, woman's 2390
  cross-stitch
    on knitting 2324
    tablecloth 2396
  dress, woman's 2398
  pattern transfers 2392, 2394, 2402, 2408

  stitch, blanket
    group 2407
    insertion 2407
    single 2407
  tablecloth 2396, 2400, 2404
Fabric, working with woven plastic 2367
Ghiordes knot 2418, 2426
Gloves, woman's knitted 2320
Hand puppets, child's sewn 2380
Hat, woman's
  crocheted 2356
  knitted 2315, 2320, 2322
Hooked rug 2416, 2418, 2422
Illustrated Sewing—see also Sewing
Illustrated Sewing 73 2360
Illustrated Sewing 74 2364
Illustrated Sewing 75 2368
Illustrated Sewing 76 2372
Inch
  conversion to centimeters 2312
  ruler 2312
Jacket
  man's crocheted 2358
  woman's
    crocheted 2356
    sewn 2364, 2370
Kalem stitch, canvaswork 2415
Knitted stitch, canvaswork 2415
Knitting
  cross-stitch on 2324
  diamond pattern 2335
  embroidery on 2324
  gloves, woman's 2320
  hat, woman's 2315, 2320, 2322
  mittens, woman's 2322
  patterns
    diamond 2335
    staggered 2330
  pullover
    man's 2317, 2328, 2331, 2334, 2336
    woman's 2315, 2318, 2324, 2326
  scarf, woman's 2320
  socks, man's 2332
  staggered pattern 2330
  tank top, man's 2334
Mat, crocheted 2338

Index

Measurements chart, body 2313
Measurements, conversion of 2312
Men
  cardigan, crocheted 2358
  jacket, crocheted 2358
  pullover, knitted 2317, 2328, 2331, 2334, 2336
  socks, knitted 2332
  tank top, knitted 2334
Metric
  conversion 2312
  ruler 2313
Mittens, woman's knitted 2322
Needlepoint—see Canvaswork
Painting design on rug canvas 2426
Patchwork
  pillow 2382, 2389
  quilt 2384
  rug
    hooked 2418
    sewn 2382
Pattern Sheet 73—dresses, child's
  adapting for additional sizes
  body measurements chart
Pattern Sheet 74—jacket, raincoat, windbreaker, woman's
  adapting for additional sizes
  body measurements chart
Pattern Sheet 75—dresses, jacket, shirt, skirt, woman's
  adapting for additional sizes
  body measurements chart
Pattern Sheet 76—blazers, skirts, vest, woman's; pillows
  adapting for additional sizes
  body measurements chart
Picture, canvaswork 2410
Pillow—see also Cushion
Pillow
  appliquéd 2386
  crocheted 2339
  hooked 2418
  patchwork 2382, 2389
  sewn 2386
Piping, inserting a corded 2362
Pullover, knitted
  man's 2317, 2328, 2331, 2334, 2336
  woman's 2315, 2318, 2324, 2326

Puppets, sewn hand 2380
Quilt, patchwork 2384
Raincoat, woman's sewn 2364
Rugmaking
  finishing 2426
  Ghiordes knot 2418, 2426
  hooked 2416, 2418, 2422
  joining canvas 2418
  painting the canvas 2426
  sewn patchwork 2382
Ruffles, crocheted 2341
Scarf, woman's knitted 2320
Sewing
  bag, bicycle 2376
  bindings, bias-cut 2370
  blazer, woman's 2372
  blouse, woman's 2390
  button fastening on a pleat 2371
  buttonhole, hand sewn 2374
  costume, child's 2378
  dress
    child's 2360
    woman's 2368, 2398
  fabric, working with woven plastic 2367
  jacket, woman's 2364, 2370
  lining a garment with self facings 2375
  patchwork
    pillow 2382, 2389
    quilt 2384
    rug 2382
  pillow 2382, 2386, 2389
  piping, inserting a corded 2362
  pleat, button fastening on a 2371
  quilt, patchwork 2384
  raincoat, woman's 2364
  rug, patchwork 2382
  shirt
    child's 2360
    woman's 2368
  skirt, woman's 2368, 2370, 2372
  suit, woman's 2370, 2372
  tablecloth 2388
  toy hand puppets 2380
  vest, woman's 2372
  windbreaker, woman's 2366
Shirt, sewn
  child's 2360
  woman's 2368
Sizing, fashion 2313

Skirt, woman's sewn 2368, 2370, 2372
Socks, man's knitted 2332
Star stitch, crocheted 2355
Strawberry pattern, crocheted 2352
Suit, woman's sewn 2370, 2372
Tablecloth
  appliquéd 2388
  border, crocheted 2404
  embroidered 2396, 2400, 2404
  sewn 2388
Tank top, man's knitted 2334
Toy hand puppets, sewn 2380
Vest, woman's
  crocheted 2347, 2349
  sewn 2372, 2374
Windbreaker, woman's sewn 2366
Women
  blazer, sewn 2372
  blouse
    embroidered 2390
    sewn 2390
  bolero, crocheted 2351
  cardigan, crocheted 2353
  dress
    embroidered 2398
    sewn 2368, 2398
  gloves, knitted 2320
  hat
    crocheted 2356
    knitted 2315, 2320, 2322
  jacket
    crocheted 2356
    sewn 2364, 2370
  mittens, knitted 2322
  pullover, knitted 2315, 2318, 2324, 2326
  raincoat, sewn 2364
  scarf, knitted 2320
  shirt, sewn 2368
  skirt, sewn 2368, 2370, 2372
  suit, sewn 2370, 2372
  vest
    crocheted 2347, 2349
    sewn 2372, 2374
  windbreaker, sewn 2366
Yarn, selecting 2312

Notes

Notes

Notes

Notes